ROBERT WILSON [barcode: KV-193-993] ns's
Grammar School, ... and at the Manchester
Grammar School. He was involved with teacher training
when working in the University of Oxford Department
of Educational Studies and has examined at Advanced
Level for the Cambridge Local Examinations Syndicate
for some years. He is now Head of the Middle School at
Aylesbury Grammar School. He is co-author of *Explore
and Express, Using English* and *Writing English*
(Macmillan). His other books include *The Brontës*
(Ward Lock Educational) and editions of Orwell's
Animal Farm and Wilde's *The Importance of Being
Earnest* (Longman).

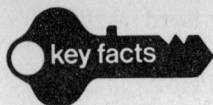

Multiple Choice

BIOLOGY, J. M. Kelly, BSc

GEOGRAPHY, BRITISH ISLES,
D. Bryant, BA and R. Knowles, MA

CHEMISTRY, C. W. Lapham, MSc

ECONOMICS, J. E. Waszek, BSc(Econ)

ENGLISH LANGUAGE, R. L. Wilson, MA

FRENCH, I. Bryden, BA

GEOGRAPHY, N. E. Law, BA

HISTORY, SOCIAL & ECONOMIC,
S. E. Haworth, BA and M. C. James, BA

HUMAN BIOLOGY, S. R. Cantle,
BSc, MMedSci

MODERN MATHEMATICS, A. J. Sly, BA

PHYSICS, B. P. Brindle, BSc

GCE O-level and CSE

English Language

R. L. Wilson, MA

key facts

Published by Charles Letts and Co Ltd
London, Edinburgh and New York

Published 1983 by Charles Letts & Co Ltd
Diary House, Borough Road, London SE1 1DW

1st edition, 1st impression
© Charles Letts & Co Ltd
Made and printed by Charles Letts (Scotland) Ltd
ISBN 0 85097 569 7

Contents

Acknowledgements

The excerpt from *The Bell* by Iris Murdoch is reprinted by permission of the author and the publishers, Chatto & Windus. The excerpt from *The Distracted Preacher,* from "Wessex Tales", by Thomas Hardy and the extract from *Journalism and Government* by John Whale are reprinted by permission of the publishers, Macmillan, London and Basingstoke.

The excerpt from *South Riding* by Winifred Holtby is included with the permission of her Literary Executor, Paul Berry.

The excerpt from *Angel Pavement* by J B Priestley is reprinted by permission of the publishers, William Heinemann Ltd.

The excerpt from *Shooting an Elephant,* from "Collected Essays, Journalism and Letters", Vol. 1, by George Orwell is reprinted by permission of the estate of the late Sonia Brownell Orwell and Martin Secker & Warburg Ltd.

The excerpt from *Daddy's Gone A-Hunting* by Penelope Mortimer is reprinted by permission of the publishers, Michael Joseph Ltd.

The excerpt from *The Trade Unions* is reprinted by permission of the author, Andrew Robertson.

The excerpt from *Rural Planning Problems* (Gordon E Cherry, ed.) is reproduced by permission of the Blackie Publishing Group.

The excerpt from *The Future of the Welfare State* by David C Marsh (Penguin Special 1964), pp. 15-17, is reprinted by permission of the publishers, Penguin Books Ltd (copyright © David C Marsh, 1964).

Chapter 1
How to Use this Book

A number of examination boards set multiple choice comprehension tests, such as you will find in this book, as part of their Ordinary Level General Certificate in Education in English Language. Multiple choice comprehensions are either set in addition to the more traditional comprehension tests, involving extended written answers, or as an alternative syllabus. All the exercises in this book are based on the different types of multiple choice questions that you will have to face if this method is used by the board that sets your examination. However, even if you do not have to do a multiple choice test in your English Language paper, you will find this book of great use in helping you to achieve the precise thinking and understanding that is necessary for dealing with the more usual comprehensions which require you to write out your answers.

That last statement may surprise you. How can doing multiple choice questions help you to deal with other, more conventional, comprehension questions? The answer relates to the type of mental skills that comprehensions of all sorts are aiming to test. They aim to test your capacity to read with understanding. The only difference between written and multiple choice comprehensions is that you have to find the words to show that you understand what you have read in the ordinary comprehension tests, whereas in multiple choice tests you must choose the answer that fits your understanding. But you must do the understanding first: answering multiple choice questions is not a guessing game enabling you to sidestep the process of coming to terms with the passage. You still have to read it in the right way. This book has been designed to help you to learn how to read different sorts of passages with appropriate attention.

Reading in the Right Way
Since the process of comprehension or understanding is the same in both multiple choice and extended writing tests, the chapters in this book have been arranged so that they can be used alongside the parallel chapters in the *Key Facts O-level Passbook* for *English Language*. In that book, Chapters 2, 3 and 4 were each concerned with a different sort of writing that you might be asked to understand

at O level. Those three chapters correspond to Chapters 2, 3 and 4 of this book. Each chapter requires you to read its passages in a different way.

In Chapter 2 – **Understanding People in Books** – you will find extracts from novels, fictional stories about people and their lives. In reading these passages, your own feelings have to come into play: you may have to sympathize with the characters, respond to how they feel about each other, try to grasp the sort of relationships that exist between the different people mentioned. You may also, and this is more difficult, have to respond to the nuances, the delicate shades of feeling that a character may be experiencing. Physical excitement, compulsion, embarrassment and calm control; love, jealousy, fear of wrong-doing and concern; guilt, anxiety, feelings of responsibility and desire for escape: these feelings are all to be found in the three extracts that constitute this chapter. Do not just read them with your mind; try to involve your feelings as well.

The third chapter – **Understanding Descriptions** – deals with facts and objective descriptions of events, or places, or the circumstances of life. You have to be alert to the detail of what the writer is describing and to the thoughts or feelings that he has about what he is presenting. The narration of an event or description of a place may give way to a reflection or thought, and that thought may then flavour the description, add a certain tone to it. In a similar way, in order to convey what a place is like, a writer will use comparisons and the comparisons may add a colour or flavour to the description. Thoughts about the lives of women in a middle-class suburban community, about the role of the white man in the East in the days of the British Empire, about the way a large restaurant is organized; comparisons between a restaurant foyer and a railway station, between house fronts and cuckoo clocks, between a crowd and a sea are all to be found in the passages in Chapter 3. When you read them, you need to keep your eye on the subject being described and be alert to all the ideas and suggestions that arise from the description.

Finally, in the fourth chapter – **Understanding Information and Argument** – you will find four pieces of writing that are mainly concerned with presenting a point of view on an issue. Here you have to absorb ideas and opinions. The writer wants to influence you so that you will come to appreciate his ideas even if you do not hold them yourself. So he includes relevant background information as part of his argument. Sometimes the argument arises out of a general presentation of the topic; sometimes the information is included as an example to illustrate the argument. In either case, you must read the passage intelligently, using your mind and asking yourself after each paragraph exactly what the author has said and how he has elaborated his ideas.

Answering a Multiple Choice Comprehension Exercise

You will by now have realized that the first rule in approaching any passage for comprehension is to read it in the right way. Give it the sort of attention that is appropriate to the intentions of the author. Understanding people, understanding descriptions and understanding information and argument are the three basic skills of reading that the exam is likely to test, and it will help you to feel far more confident if you can sense the type of passage you are reading quite soon after you have begun to read it.

When you tackle a question, go back to the passage to remind yourself of the content of the part of the passage to which the question refers. Work out a completion of the statement in your own mind before you look at the alternatives presented to you. When you have some idea of how you think the statement should be completed, look at the alternatives in front of you and consider each one carefully. Do not worry about the length of time you spend doing this. Think through each alternative in an orderly manner: it will not take you long to write down the answer once you have decided upon it. If you are really in doubt, try eliminating the alternatives that seem more obviously inappropriate.

At the back of the book, answers are provided. Do the whole exercise on a passage before you turn to the answers. There really is no point in cheating yourself. Where appropriate, commentaries have been included, giving arguments for choosing the correct answer or explaining why the others are wrong. When you have completed a comprehension exercise, you will learn much by spending some time in going through the answer section and referring back to the passage to check the thinking that should have led you to the correct choice, especially in those cases where you have answered wrongly.

Chapter 2
Understanding People in Books

In approaching the sort of passage in this chapter, you may well
find that it helps to read right through the extract a couple of times
taking in as much of the detail as you can, noticing how many
people there are in the passage, what their names are and what
relationships they have with each other. Then, when you have put
the situation or incident into perspective and have a sense of what
it is all about, you will be in a better position to deal with a more
difficult task, that of understanding the feelings and motives and
possibly the changing emotions of the people involved. The first
three questions on the first passage in this chapter are designed to
help you put the whole situation into perspective and understand
who is involved.

A Toby Goes Exploring

When climbing the wall Toby had not meant to do more than
look into the Abbey grounds. Now that he was on the wall he
began to feel, tickling and torturing him as a physical urge,
the desire to jump down into the enclosure. A moment or two
5 after feeling the urge he knew it to be irresistible. He might
delay but sooner or later he *must* jump. When he realized this
he became so agitated that he jumped immediately, landing
with a good deal of noise and damage to his clothing among
some brambles. He picked himself up and stood still, breath-
10 ing hard and listening. As everything remained quiet he
moved cautiously away from the wall and walked softly
towards the alley where he hoped he might get a view of the
Abbey buildings.

Trembling a little and feeling that at any moment a stern
15 voice might call him to account, Toby came into the open
ground at the end of the alley. The alley was smooth and well
kept. It led, however, not to a building but to another smaller
wall in which there was a door. Nothing more could be seen.
Toby stood still for a while looking. He wondered what
20 would happen if he were found; and his imagination hesitated
between a picture of nuns fleeing from him with piercing
screams and nuns leaping upon him like bacchantes.* He did
not know which picture was the more alarming; or indeed, he
was amazed to find himself reflecting, the more delicious.

25 Gradually as he stood there in the unnerving silence of the place his dismay at what he had done increased. He decided he had better start climbing back again. However the repetition, further down the alley, of the wall and the door constituted too fascinating a challenge. He could not take his
30 eyes off the door; and in a moment he found himself gliding between the trees towards it.

When he reached it he looked back. Already the high wall of the enclosure seemed far away. He reflected that he might yet have to return at a run. He faced the little door. The wall here
35 was lower, but too high to see over. It disappeared into the shade of trees on either side; but there were no trees beyond the wall. The avenue ended at this point. Toby put his hand on the latch and took a deep breath. He pressed the latch down and the bar rose with a loud click. He pressed the door
40 which groaned a little and began to open slowly. The noise alarmed him, but he went on pushing the door which opened onto a carpet of close-cut grass. He stepped through the opening and found himself in a cemetery.

The unexpectedness of the scene made Toby rigid in the
45 doorway, his hand still on the door. He was in a green space enclosed by a rectangle of walls, within which there stretched neatly row after row of graves, each with a small white cross above it. A line of rather gaunt black cypresses against the sun-baked wall on the far side gave the place a strangely southern
50 aspect. His alarm at the vision was hardly increased by seeing quite near to him two nuns who were apparently tending the graves. One of them had a pair of shears in her hand. A lawn mower stood by but had evidently not been in use or Toby would have heard it. Toby looked at the nuns and the nuns,
55 who had straightened up from their labours at the sound of the opening gate, looked at Toby.

The nun with the shears laid down her tool and said something in a low voice to the second nun. Then she came towards Toby, her long habit sweeping the grass. Paralysed with
60 shame and alarm he watched her approach.

When she was near enough for him to focus his distracted glance upon her face he saw that she was smiling. His hand dropped from the gate and he stepped back automatically out of the cemetery. She followed him, closing the gate

65 behind her, and they faced each other in the alley.

"Good morning," said the nun. "I believe you must be Toby. Have I guessed right?"

"Yes," said Toby, hanging his head.

They began to walk slowly back together between the trees.
70 "I thought so," said the nun. "Although we never meet, we seem to know each one of you, as if you were our dearest friends." The nun seemed quite at her ease. Toby was in an agony of embarrassment and alarm.

"I expect our little cemetery gave you quite a surprise?" said
75 the nun.

"It did!" said Toby.

"It's a beautiful place, don't you think?" said the nun. "It's so cosy and enclosed, rather like a dormitory I sometimes think. It's nice to know that one will sleep there oneself one day."

80 "It's beautiful, yes," said Toby, desperate.

They passed under a large cedar tree from whose spreading lower branches Toby noticed something hanging. It was a swing. Involuntarily he reached out his hand as he neared it and touched the rope.

85 "It's a fine swing," said the nun. Her voice was by now betraying her as Irish. "Why not try it? It would cheer the old swing up. We sometimes do ourselves."

Toby hesitated. Then blushing violently he sat in the swing and urged himself several times to and fro. The nun stood by
90 smiling.

Mumbling something Toby got out of the swing. He was ready to run, to dive into the ground. Averting his head he walked on beside the nun, who was still talking, until they reached the gate in the enclosure wall.

95 The nun opened the gate.

13

"It wasn't locked!" said Toby with surprise.

"Why, we never bother locking the gates!" said the nun. "I
expect you enjoyed your climb. Young boys are forever
climbing things." Beaming she swung the gate open. Toby
100 stepped through and for a moment they looked at each other
through the gateway. Toby felt he ought to apologize and
struggled for the words.

"I'm sorry," he said. "I know I oughtn't to have come in."

"Don't be after worrying," said the nun. "They say that
105 curiosity killed the cat, but I never believed it when I was
your age. Besides, we have a special rule which says that
children can som'etimes come into the enclosure." She closed
the gate between them and it seemed to Toby that her smile
lingered on the outside of the gate for a second or two after
110 it clicked shut. He turned to face the avenue.

All was silent. No one had seen his entry and no one had seen
his ignominious exit. He began to run down the avenue,
anxious to get as far away as possible from the dangerous and
it now seemed to him even more impregnable enclosure. He
115 felt ridiculous, humiliated and ashamed. He ran with his head
down saying, "Damn, damn, damn," to himself as he went
along.

from The Bell by Iris Murdoch

* *bacchantes* – priestesses of the Greek god Bacchus. Here
the word means women enjoying drunken revelry.

Each of the following questions consists of an incomplete statement or question followed by four or five suggested completions.
You are to select the most appropriate completion in each case.

1 From your reading of the whole passage would you say that
   Toby was
   A younger than 9 years old
   B aged between 9 and 13
   C aged between 13 and 18 –
   D older than 18

2 From your reading of the whole passage, do you understand

the enclosure into which he jumps to be
A   the grounds of an abbey closed to the public
B   the grounds of a country house that was once a nunnery
    but has ceased to be now
C   a private cemetery
D   the grounds of a country house containing a film set

3 The reception Toby received from the nun was
A   hostile and rejecting
B   patronizing
C   cool and indifferent
D   friendly but firmly excluding

4 Toby jumped down from the wall because
A   he was frightened by a noise
B   he knew he could not resist his own curiosity
C   he was tickled and then pushed from behind
D   he itched and began to slip

5 "Agitated" (line 7) means that Toby was
A   excited inside himself
B   jumping up and down on the wall
C   fearful of falling
D   unable to decide what to do

6 "Feeling that at any moment a stern voice might call him to
account" (line 14) suggests that Toby
A   had not paid the required entrance fee
B   had noticed he was being watched and would be asked
    what he was doing
C   felt his life had been sinful and was expecting judgement
D   knew he was doing wrong and felt guilty

7 In the second paragraph, which **two** of the following scenes
occur in Toby's imagination? He imagines
    1 nuns playing innocently with him
    2 nuns running away from him in great fear
    3 nuns falling all over him in riotous delight
    4 nuns sternly telling him to leave
    A   1 and 3 only
    B   1 and 4 only
    C   2 and 3 only
    D   2 and 4 only
    E   3 and 4 only

8 Which **three** feelings did Toby experience as a result of imagining how the nuns would react to him? The feelings produced in Toby by his imagination were
    1 surprise
    2 pleasure
    3 reassurance
    4 concern
    5 fright
        A 1, 2 and 3 only
        B 1, 2 and 5 only
        C 1, 2 and 4 only
        D 2, 3 and 4 only
        E 2, 3 and 5 only

9 "Unnerving silence" (line 25) implies that the silence made Toby feel
    A that he had no nervous feelings
    B that he was deceiving people
    C that he was in a hopeless situation
    D that he had lost all his boldness

10 The statement "the door constituted too fascinating a challenge" (line 28), implies most closely that the door was
    A a temptation that Toby could not resist
    B too strongly framed in the wall for Toby to open it
    C so intricate that Toby must keep looking at it
    D so interesting to Toby that he wanted to break it down

11 When he reached the door Toby looked back (line 32) because
    A he thought he had heard a noise behind him
    B he wanted to avoid having to open the door
    C he wanted to see how far he had penetrated into the enclosure
    D he wanted more time to think about what he was doing

12 As he opened the door, Toby was aware of all the following EXCEPT
    A the sound of the door as it opened
    B his fear
    C the clicking sound of the latch
    D the furious beating of his heart

13 "Gaunt" (line 48) is best defined as

16

    A thin
    B flourishing
    C colourful
    D mysterious

14 "A strangely southern aspect" (line 49) means that the place
    A faced south
    B was unexpectedly sunny
    C looked surprisingly like places in the south of Europe
    D could be seen when looked at from an odd angle

15 When Toby appeared in the cemetery, one of the nuns reacted
   in all the following ways EXCEPT
    A laying down her gardening tool
    B speaking to the other nun
    C smiling at Toby
    D sweeping her arm round so as to cause Toby to withdraw

16 The word "distracted" (line 61) means that Toby was
    A looking straight at the nun all the time
    B confused about what he was seeing
    C avoiding the eye of the nun
    D interrupting the labour of the nuns by looking at them

17 According to lines 66 to 80, Toby felt all the following
   EXCEPT
    A fear
    B hopelessness
    C shame
    D peace

18 It is most likely that the nun invited Toby to use the swing
   (line 86) in order to
    A help him relax
    B make him feel childish
    C keep him longer in the enclosure
    D make him embarrassed

19 The nun mentions the "special rule" about children in line 106
   in order to
    A make Toby feel inferior
    B invite him to come again
    C excuse her own conduct in talking to him
    D imply that what he has done is excusable

20 What **two** things does Toby want to do when he leaves the enclosure? He wants to
   1 get away from the place
   2 curse the monastery for humiliating and excluding him
   3 condemn himself for putting himself in an embarrassing situation
   4 break into the enclosure again as soon as he can
   5 find some one safe since no one was around
   A 1 and 2 only
   B 1 and 3 only
   C 1 and 5 only
   D 2 and 4 only
   E 3 and 5 only

B The Proposal

Matters being in this advancing state, Stockdale was rather surprised one cloudy evening, while sitting in his room, at hearing her speak in low tones of expostulation to some one at the door. It was nearly dark, but the shutters were not yet
5 closed, nor the candles lighted; and Stockdale was tempted to stretch his head towards the window. He saw outside the door a young man in clothes of a whitish colour, and upon reflection judged their wearer to be the well-built and rather handsome miller who lived below. The miller's voice was
10 alternately low and firm, and sometimes it reached the level of positive entreaty; but what the words were Stockdale could in no way hear.

Before the colloquy had ended, the minister's attention was attracted by a second incident. Opposite Lizzie's home grew
15 a clump of laurels, forming a thick and permanent shade. One of the laurel boughs now quivered against the light background of sky, and in a moment the head of a man peered out, and remained still. He seemed to be also much interested in the conversation at the door, and was plainly lingering
20 there to watch and listen. Had Stockdale stood in any other relation to Lizzie but that of a lover, he might have gone out and investigated the meaning of this: but being as yet but an unprivileged ally, he did nothing more than stand up and show himself against the firelight, whereupon the listener
25 disappeared, and Lizzie and the miller spoke in lower tones.

Stockdale was made so uneasy by the circumstance, that as soon as the miller was gone, he said, "Mrs. Newberry, are you aware that you were watched just now, and your conversation heard?"

30 "When?" she said.

"When you were talking to that miller. A man was looking from the laurel-tree as jealously as if he could have eaten you."

She showed more concern than the trifling event seemed to demand, and he added, "Perhaps you were talking of things
35 you did not wish to be overheard?"

"I was talking only on business," she said.

"Lizzie, be frank!" said the young man. "If it was only on business, why should anybody wish to listen to you?"

She looked curiously at him. "What else do you think it could
40 be, then?"

"Well – the only talk between a young woman and man that is likely to amuse an eavesdropper."

"Ah yes," she said, smiling in spite of her preoccupation. "Well my cousin Owlett has spoken to me about matrimony,
45 every now and then, that's true; but he was not speaking of it then. I wish he had been speaking of it with all my heart. It would have been much less serious for me."

"O Mrs. Newberry!"

"It would. Not that I should ha' chimed in with him, of course.
50 I wish it for other reasons. I am glad, Mr. Stockdale, that you told me of that listener. It is a timely warning, and I must see my cousin again."

"But don't go away till I have spoken," said the minister. "I'll out with it at once, and make no more ado. Let it be Yes or No
55 between us, Lizzie; please do!" And he held out his hand, in which she freely allowed her own to rest, but without speaking.

"You mean Yes by that?" he asked, after waiting a while.

"You may be my sweetheart, if you will."

19

"Why not say at once you will wait for me until I have a house
60 and can come back to marry you?"

"Because I am thinking – thinking of something else," she
said with embarrassment. "It all comes upon me at once,
and I must settle one thing at a time."

"At any rate, dear Lizzie, you can assure me that the miller
65 shall not be allowed to speak to you except on business? You
have never directly encouraged him?"

She parried the question by saying, "You see, he and his
party have been in the habit of leaving things on my premises
sometimes, and as I have not denied him, it makes him rather
70 forward."

"Things – what things?"

"Tubs – they are called Things here."

"But why don't you deny him, my dear Lizzie?"

"I cannot well."

75 "You are too timid. It is unfair of him to impose so upon you,
and get your good name into danger by his smuggling tricks.
Promise me that the next time he wants to leave his tubs here
you will let me roll them into the street?"

She shook her head. "I would not venture to offend the
80 neighbours so much as that," said she, "or do anything that
would be likely to put poor Owlett into the hands of the
customs-men."

Stockdale sighed, and said that he thought hers a mistaken
generosity when it extended to assisting those who cheated
85 the king of his dues. "At any rate, you will let me make him
keep his distance as your lover, and tell him flatly that you are
not for him?"

"Please not, at present," she said, "I don't wish to offend my
old neighbours. It is not only Mr. Owlett who is concerned."

90 "This is too bad," said Stockdale impatiently.

"On my honour, I won't encourage him as my lover," Lizzie answered earnestly. "A reasonable man will be satisfied with that."

"Well, so I am," said Stockdale, his countenance clearing.

from *The Distracted Preacher* by Thomas Hardy

1 Stockdale's occupation in the village was that of
   A   miller
   B   minister
   C   customs-man
   D   dairy-farmer

2 Stockdale's relationship with Lizzie Newberry was that of
   A   husband
   B   fiancé
   C   brother
   D   sweetheart

3 Owlett wanted to talk to Lizzie because
   A   they were both engaged in smuggling
   B   they were cousins and had family business to talk about
   C   he was trying to get Lizzie to marry him
   D   they had secretly agreed to marry and had to make arrangements

4 The word "expostulation" in line 3 is nearest in meaning to
   A   wooing
   B   violent denunciation
   C   urging
   D   angry condemnation

5 What **two** characteristics did Stockdale notice about the way the miller spoke to Lizzie (lines 9-12)? The miller sounded as if he were
   1   talking in the same tone all the time
   2   sometimes raising his voice to urge a point forcefully
   3   always very positive in his requests
   4   sometimes quiet and other times firm
      A   1 and 2 only
      B   3 and 4 only
      C   1 and 3 only
      D   2 and 4 only

21

6 The word "colloquy" in line 13 means
   A evening
   B conversation
   C twilight
   D row

7 The phrase "unprivileged ally" in line 23 implies that
   A Stockdale was just a friend who wanted to be helpful to
      Lizzie
   B Stockdale was involved with the smuggling but did not get
      much income from it
   C the eavesdropper behind the laurels had no right to be
      there
   D Stockdale had not yet been invited to join the smugglers
      but he wanted to

8 We are told that when he noticed the eavesdropper Stockdale
   felt all the following EXCEPT
   A interest in why the eavesdropper was there
   B desire to scare the eavesdropper away
   C awareness of how limited was his relationship with Lizzie
   D desire to forget all about it

9 It is most likely that Lizzie Newberry "showed more concern
   than the trifling event seemed to demand" (line 33)
   because
   A she had been discussing matrimony with Owlett
   B she thought Stockdale would report her to the customs-men
   C she thought the eavesdropper may have been a customs-man
   D she was annoyed that Stockdale had been watching her

10 The phrase "in spite of her preoccupation" (line 43) suggests
   that Lizzie was
   A thinking of something else
   B remembering how she used to live
   C feeling very angry
   D feeling guilty about how she made her living

11 Stockdale thinks Owlett and Lizzie have been talking about
   A youth
   B smuggling
   C love
   D business

22

12 Stockdale made all the following requests of Lizzie EXCEPT
   A that she would marry him
   B that she would let him join the smugglers
   C that she would not allow Owlett to woo her
   D that she would refuse to be involved in the smuggling in future

13 In saying, "It would have been much less serious for me" (line 47), Lizzie implied
   A she did not think that marriage was a serious subject
   B she wished she had been overheard discussing marriage rather than smuggling
   C she felt that marriage to Owlett would be less solemn than marriage to Stockdale
   D she wanted to marry Stockdale rather than Owlett

14 When Stockdale asked if Lizzie would marry him (line 54), she
   A changed the subject at once
   B agreed
   C declined
   D encouraged him to some extent

15 The word closest in meaning to "parried" in line 67 is
   A averted
   B altered
   C played
   D answered

16 "Things" in line 71 were probably
   A guns
   B tubs of flour
   C tubs of alcoholic liquor
   D electrical goods

17 Stockdale felt that Lizzie might lose her good name (line 76) by
   A being thought a loose woman
   B marrying her cousin
   C becoming known as an accomplice of the smugglers
   D being denounced to the police by Owlett

18 "Those who cheated the king of his dues" may best be defined as
   A people who refused to honour the king

B people who avoided paying taxes
C people who did not pay properly for services provided by the government
D people who wanted a republic

19 Lizzie said she did not want to stop helping Owlett because
A there were other people who also depended on her
B she secretly loved Owlett
C there was no one else to help him
D she approved of smuggling

20 At the end of the conversation, Stockdale was happier because
A Lizzie agreed not to help the smugglers
B she agreed to marry him
C she gave him her hand
D she agreed to discourage Owlett's matrimonial advances

C Sarah Burton Examines Her Conscience

With quick precision Sarah opened her letters, cutting the envelopes neatly, sorting their contents – business, receipts, bills, estimates and the rest of them – letters from parents or staff about school vacancies – personal communications. She
5 received fewer and fewer of this third category. She had become increasingly absorbed in her professional affairs. She neglected her friends. The school, the school, the school filled her deliberate mind. "You're becoming a mono-maniac," Pattie had told her.

10 There was one envelope addressed in a slanting scholarly hand which was familiar. Sarah unfolded the thin blue paper and read:

> 26a Canning Terrace,
> Tunbridge Wells,
15   March 13th, 1934.

"My Dear Miss Burton,"

It was from Miss Sigglesthwaite. A wave of nausea rocked in Sarah's mind. She still felt that she had treated Miss Siggles-thwaite shabbily. She had given her rope to hang herself,
20 longing to replace her. She had sacrificed her and secured her efficient Miss Vane, fresh from Cambridge. She had let her

become the victim of bad mass-bullying, and had left un-
punished the ringleader of her tormentors.

With stern self-discipline Sarah compelled herself to read the
25 letter.

"My Dear Miss Burton,
You may doubtless be wondering why you have not heard
from me. I apologise for any lack of courtesy, but knowing
your kind thoughts for me I waited till I had cheerful news to
30 send.
"I can now report that my own health has already shown
great improvement, and that I have found another post.
"I am now installed as daily companion to an elderly lady
living here who is almost blind. I conduct her correspondence
35 for her, read to her, and wheel her out when it is fine in a bath
chair. You would be amused at her literary tastes, and so am
I. I shall soon become an expert in the works of Ruby M.
Ayres, Pamela Wynne and Ursula Bloom. Do you know any
of these novelists? I assure you that they have opened up a
40 new world to me. My salary is not princely, but as I can live at
home, we have been able to give up our maid and my sister
does the housework while I relieve her at night, by looking
after our poor mother, so I think with care we shall be able to
manage if we can both retain our health.
45 "And now, my dear Miss Burton, may I at last be allowed to
thank you, not only for your extreme kindness to me after my
breakdown, but for your more than generous and heartening
letter which arrived last week? Please believe me that I shall
never forget your patience with my shortcomings; and your
50 sympathy when they proved at last too much for me. I realise
that I should have retired earlier, but you know my circumstances, and I am more than grateful that you never uttered
one word of reproach.
"I shall always watch from afar your career in the world of
55 teaching with the warmest interest, remembering how, in
your youth and vigour you found generosity enough to show
kindness to my stupidity and failure. I feel sure that you will
go far and I shall always rejoice in your well-deserved success.
"Believe me, yours gratefully and sincerely,
60   "AGNES SIGGLESTHWAITE."

Sarah laid the letter on her desk, and sat staring out to the
sea. A fishing smack with a brown sail dipped and tossed

25

there and sometimes disappeared. Sarah held her breath till
it re-emerged, but she was not really thinking of it. She was
65 picturing the tall lank woman pushing her employer about in
a bath chair through the streets of Tunbridge Wells, her hair
pins tinkling behind her to the pavement, her skirt un-
buttoned, her jumper gaping above her waist belt, her mild
chin quivering below her sensitive mouth. She could hear her
70 cultured voice pronouncing with its habitual precision the
declaration of love, the luxurious descriptions of feminine
underwear, the conflicts of vice with virtue, so frequently
encountered in her employer's favourite literature.

"So there goes the most distinguished scientist we have ever
75 had on our staff – or ever will have," she thought, and her
heart rebuked her.

The simple generosity and goodness of Agnes Sigglesthwaite
were too much for her. She had become morbidly self-
reproachful for her part in that affair. She had lain awake
80 telling herself that she had sacrificed the science mistress for
Midge Carne, that it was Midge whom she should have sent
away, that the child was hysterical, vain, a centre of exaggerated emotion, an unhealthy influence in the school.

She forgot the weeks when she had sheltered Miss Siggles-
85 thwaite in her own house, sitting with her at night and reading
to her, pouring into her exhausted mind the optimism and
resilience of her own unstaled philosophy. She forgot her
unstinted efforts to beat the sickness and sorrow of the over-
burdened woman. She only remembered that her kindness
90 had been mingled with impatience, her benevolence soured
by her planning mind.

"A companion to a blind lady who lives here." And it's my
fault, she groaned in spirit. She put the letter in the basket
marked "to be answered", and picked up the next one.

95 But the telephone rang, and when she lifted the receiver she
heard her friend Joe Astell calling to her in his hoarse and
breathless voice.

It brought some comfort to her. The knowledge of his
sympathy and support had meant much to her during the past
100 difficult weeks. She knew that he liked and respected her, and

his appreciation helped her to retain a modicum of her own self-respect.

from *South Riding* by Winifred Holtby

1 Miss Sarah Burton is employed at the Kiplington High School for girls as
  A Senior Science Mistress
  B Deputy Head
  C Headmistress
  D School Secretary

2 From the way she deals with her mail (lines 1-5), we learn that Miss Burton has all the following qualities EXCEPT
  A efficiency
  B decisiveness
  C capacity for fast work
  D unfriendliness

3 The three dashes in lines 2-4 could all correctly be replaced by
  A commas
  B brackets
  C semi-colons
  D colons

4 The word "monomaniac" (line 8) tells us that Pattie thinks Miss Burton is
  A too much on her own
  B obsessed with power
  C too preoccupied with the school
  D going mad

5 "given her rope to hang herself" (line 19) is an expression which is
  A slang
  B exaggerated
  C sarcastic
  D metaphoric

6 When she opens Miss Sigglesthwaite's letter (lines 10-23), Miss Burton blames herself for all the following reasons EXCEPT
  A she had treated Miss Sigglesthwaite badly
  B she had given Miss Sigglesthwaite's job to a young and inadequate teacher

C she had allowed Miss Sigglesthwaite to destroy herself
D she had been unjust

7 The novels that Miss Sigglesthwaite reads to her employer
(lines 37-38) are *mainly* about
A women's fashions
B romantic love
C science fiction
D moral conflict

8 Agnes Sigglesthwaite's previous post had been that of
A Science Mistress
B Headmistress
C companion to an old lady
D university lecturer

9 Agnes Sigglesthwaite has written to Miss Burton *primarily* to
A thank Miss Burton for her previous help
B tell her about her difficult financial situation
C give an amusing account of her new way of life
D send news that will cheer up Miss Burton

10 When she has finished reading Miss Sigglesthwaite's letter,
Miss Burton *mainly* feels
A absent-minded
B guilty
C intrigued by Miss Sigglesthwaite's new life
D admiration for Miss Sigglesthwaite

11 That Miss Burton's philosophy was "unstaled" (line 87) means
that it was
A old
B rejuvenating
C reliable
D fresh and youthful

12 "unstinted" (line 88) may be most accurately replaced by
A casual
B unrestricted
C vigorous
D generous

13 The full-stop after "affair" (line 79) could equally well be
replaced by

28

A   a colon
B   a semi-colon
C   a comma
D   a dash

14 Miss Burton's mind was always "planning" (line 91)
    A   to get rid of Miss Sigglesthwaite
    B   to be hard with people
    C   to improve the education in the school
    D   things to do with the future

15 All the following adjectives could justifiably be applied to Miss Sigglesthwaite EXCEPT
    A   generous
    B   reproachful
    C   untidy
    D   cultured

16 All of the following inferences about Miss Burton's treatment of Miss Sigglesthwaite may be drawn from the paragraph beginning on line 84 EXCEPT that she
    A   tried to support Miss Sigglesthwaite
    B   was not always concentrating on Miss Sigglesthwaite
    C   had generally been impatient
    D   had attempted to cheer up the unhappy woman

17 "she groaned in spirit" (line 93) may most appropriately be replaced by
    A   she groaned in a lively way
    B   she sighed in her mind
    C   she murmured quietly
    D   she felt ill from drink

18 Midge Carne (line 81) was
    A   a girl who had a hold over Miss Burton
    B   a teacher who took Miss Sigglesthwaite's job
    C   a sick child who caused an epidemic
    D   a girl who tormented Miss Sigglesthwaite

19 Miss Burton feels comforted at hearing Joe Astell's voice (line 96) because
    A   he is her friend
    B   she needs a man to support her
    C   he helps her feel good about herself
    D   she likes the hoarse sound of his voice

20 The author's main judgement about Miss Burton is that she
  A is to be condemned for her treatment of Miss Sigglesthwaite
  B is too ready to condemn herself
  C is neither good nor bad in her job
  D was right to replace Miss Sigglesthwaite

Chapter 3
Understanding Descriptions

Three different sorts of description are included in this chapter. The first passage describes with great care and precision a sequence of events that the author has experienced. He concentrates on exactly what happened on this one particular occasion rather than on details of the surroundings. He is not trying to make us have certain feelings about the event, though doubtless every reader does have feelings about the killing of the elephant; rather, he is concerned to allow the facts of what happened to speak for themselves.

In the second passage, you will be far more aware of the tone, the humour that JB Priestley infuses into his description of the sort of café that was popular in England in the twenties and thirties but which has died out since the Second World War. The surroundings are important in this passage and are conveyed through lists of details and through many comparisons, some of which you will be asked to examine.

The third passage of this chapter is not concerned with one incident nor with a single impression of a place. It is a more general description dealing with the way of life of a particular area known as "the Common". Rather than convey events that took place on one occasion, the passage describes the pattern of life for men, women and children in the area on a typical Sunday morning.

A Shooting an Elephant
I had halted on the road. As soon as I saw the elephant I knew with perfect certainty that I ought not to shoot him. It is a serious matter to shoot a working elephant – it is comparable to destroying a huge and costly piece of machinery –
5 and obviously one ought not to do it if it can possibly be avoided. And at that distance, peacefully eating, the elephant looked no more dangerous than a cow. I thought then and I think now that his attack of "must" * was already passing off, in which case he would merely wander harmlessly
10 about until the mahout† came back and caught him. Moreover, I did not in the least want to shoot him. I decided that I would watch for a little to make sure that he did not turn savage again, and then go home.

But at that moment I glanced round at the crowd that had
15 followed me. It was an immense crowd, two thousand at the
least and growing every minute. It blocked the road for a long
distance on either side. I looked at the sea of yellow faces
above the garish clothes – faces all happy and excited over
this bit of fun, all certain that the elephant was going to be
20 shot. They were watching me as they would watch a conjurer
about to perform a trick. They did not like me, but with the
magic rifle in my hands I was momentarily worth watching.
And suddenly I realised that I would have to shoot the
elephant after all. The people expected it of me and I had got
25 to do it; I could feel their two thousand wills pressing me
forward, irresistibly. And it was at this moment, as I stood
there with the rifle in my hands, that I first grasped the
hollowness, the futility of the white man's dominion in
the East. Here was I, the white man with his gun, standing in
30 front of the unarmed native crowd – seemingly the leading
actor of the piece; but in reality I was only an absurd puppet
pushed to and fro by the will of those yellow faces behind ....

But I did not want to shoot the elephant. I watched him
beating his bunch of grass against his knees, with that pre-
35 occupied grandmotherly air that elephants have. It seemed to
me that it would be murder to shoot him. At that age I was
not squeamish about killing animals, but I had never shot an
elephant and never wanted to. (Somehow it always seems
worse to kill a *large* animal.) Besides, there was the beast's
40 owner to be considered. Alive, the elephant was worth at
least a hundred pounds: dead, he would only be worth the
value of his tusks, five pounds, possibly. But I had got to act
quickly. I turned to some experienced-looking Burmans who
had been there when we arrived, asked them how the
45 elephant had been behaving. They all said the same thing: he
took no notice of you if you left him alone, but he might
charge if you went too close to him.

It was perfectly clear what I ought to do. I ought to walk up to
within, say, twenty-five yards of the elephant and test his
50 behaviour. If he charged, I could shoot, if he took no notice
of me it would be safe to leave him until the mahout came
back. But also I knew that I was going to do no such thing. I
was a poor shot with a rifle and the ground was soft mud into
which one would sink at every step. If the elephant charged
55 and I missed him, I would have about as much chance as a

toad under a steam-roller. But even then I was not thinking particularly of my own skin, only of the watchful yellow faces behind. For at that moment, with the crowd watching me, I was not afraid in the ordinary sense, as I would have been if I 60 had been alone. A white man mustn't be frightened in front of 'natives'; and so, in general, he isn't frightened. The sole thought in my mind was that if anything went wrong these two thousand Burmans would see me pursued, caught, trampled on and reduced to a grinning corpse like that Indian 65 up the hill. And if that happened it was quite probable that some of them would laugh. That would never do. There was only one alternative. I shoved the cartridges into the magazine and lay down on the road to get a better aim.

The crowd grew very still, and a deep, low, happy sigh, as of 70 people who see the theatre curtain go up at last, breathed from innumerable throats. They were going to have their bit of fun after all. The rifle was a beautiful German thing with cross-hair sights. I did not then know that in shooting an elephant one should shoot to cut an imaginary bar running 75 from ear-hole to ear-hole. I ought, therefore, as the elephant was sideways on, to have aimed straight at his ear-hole; actually I aimed several inches in front of this, thinking the brain would be further forward.

When I pulled the trigger I did not hear the bang or feel the 80 kick – one never does when a shot goes home – but I heard the devilish roar of glee that went up from the crowd. In that instant, in too short a time, one would have thought, even for the bullet to get there, a mysterious, terrible change had come over the elephant. He neither stirred nor fell, but every 85 line of his body had altered. He looked suddenly stricken, shrunken, immensely old, as though the frightful impact of the bullet had paralysed him without knocking him down. At last, after what seemed a long time – it might have been five seconds, I dare say – he sagged flabbily to his knees. His 90 mouth slobbered. An enormous senility seemed to have settled upon him. One could have imagined him thousands of years old. I fired again into the same spot. At the second shot he did not collapse but climbed with desperate slowness to his feet and stood weakly upright, with legs sagging and 95 head drooping. I fired a third time. That was the shot that did for him. You could see the agony of it jolt his whole body and knock the last remnant of strength from his legs. But in

33

falling he seemed for a moment to rise, for as his hind legs collapsed beneath him he seemed to tower upwards like a
100 huge rock toppling, his trunk reaching skywards like a tree. He trumpeted, for the first and only time. And then down he came, his belly towards me, with a crash that seemed to shake the ground even where I lay.

from *Shooting an Elephant* by George Orwell

* *must* – an attack of madness in an elephant.
† *mahout* – a man who looks after an elephant.

1 In the first paragraph the author says he did not want to kill the elephant for all the following reasons EXCEPT
  A the elephant was too valuable to be destroyed
  B . he was frightened the elephant might charge him
  C the elephant had completely recovered from his attack of madness
  D the elephant appeared completely harmless

2 At the end of the first paragraph the author records his decision to
  A postpone killing the elephant until later
  B watch the elephant for a while and then kill him
  C avoid killing the elephant whatever happened
  D make sure that the elephant remained peaceful and then leave him

3 Which **three** of the following qualities are likely to have been in the author's mind when he described an elephant as "a huge and costly piece of machinery" (line 4)? The author was probably thinking that an elephant
    1 is as useful to man as is a piece of machinery
    2 needs food just as a machine needs oil
    3 is as complex and wonderfully made as a machine
    4 is sometimes as unreliable as a machine that breaks down
    5 is as costly to purchase and as valuable to have as a great machine
      A 1, 2 and 3 only
      B 1, 4 and 5 only
      C 1, 3 and 5 only
      D 2, 3 and 4 only
      E 3, 4 and 5 only

4 When the crowd is described as watching the author "as they would watch a conjurer about to perform a trick" (line 20), it is mainly implied that the people
A hoped to see a miracle performed by the author
B wanted to see the author make a mistake
C expected a bit of entertainment
D thought the author was cheap and disliked his tricking them

5 The author realized that he "would have to shoot the elephant after all" (line 23) because
A he would have to do what all the people wanted
B he enjoyed being the centre of attention
C he was a good shot
D the elephant really was dangerous

6 "the futility of the white man's dominion in the East" (line 28) most closely suggests that
A white men ought to keep struggling to achieve lordship in the East
B white races will not gain any wealth from the East
C it is pointless for white men to attempt to achieve lordship in the East
D it is wrong to dominate other peoples

7 In order to bring out his feeling of powerlessness the author compares himself in the second paragraph with
A a conjurer
B a puppet
C a sea
D an actor

8 The word "garish" (line 18) is best defined as
A over-decorated
B colourful
C varied
D attractive

9 "I was not squeamish" (line 36) most closely suggests that the author
A enjoyed killing animals
B hated killing animals
C was not sickened by the idea of killing animals
D had no feelings about killing animals

10 "no such thing" (line 52) refers to
   A approaching the elephant to kill him at close range
   B leaving the elephant alone without more ado
   C finding out how the elephant would behave if someone walked close to him
   D the author's inability to shoot well

11 The author places "natives" (line 61) inside single inverted commas because
   A he is not familiar with the word
   B he does not think his readers will understand the word
   C he is using a slang word
   D he wants the reader to think about the associations of the word

12 The author decided not to go close and test the elephant's behaviour (line 52) for all the following reasons EXCEPT that
   A he was not very accurate when using a rifle
   B if the elephant charged he would not escape
   C he was afraid of being trampled
   D he did not want to look ridiculous

13 As the author prepared to shoot, the crowd's reaction is described in all the following ways EXCEPT
   A quietened
   B amused
   C contented
   D full of anticipation

14 The author ought to have aimed at a different part of the elephant's head in order to
   A avoid hitting a bar across his forehead
   B deafen the elephant
   C drive the bullet into the brain
   D wound the elephant without killing him

15 We are told that the author did not hear the bang of the rifle (line 79) because
   A it was a good shot
   B the bang was drowned by the roar of the crowd
   C he was preoccupied with the kick of the rifle
   D he was too worried about whether he had killed the elephant

16 The phrase "too short a time" (line 82) refers to
   A the speed with which the author made up his mind to shoot
   B the time taken by the bullet to reach the elephant
   C the violent reaction of the crowd
   D the rapid deterioration of the elephant

17 "senility" (line 90) is best defined as
   A aging
   B feebleness
   C sagging
   D withering

18 The "mysterious, terrible change" (line 83) that occurred
   immediately after the first shot was fired was the elephant's
   A collapse to his knees
   B sudden aging
   C standing still
   D desperate attempt to get up

19 After the third shot, the elephant reacted in all the following
   ways EXCEPT
   A by making a great noise
   B by crashing to the ground
   C by kicking out with his legs
   D by registering the pain through his entire body

20 Which **two** of the following qualities are likely to have been in
   the author's mind when he compared the elephant with "a
   huge rock toppling" (line 100)? The comparison suggests
   1 how much damage he would do when he fell
   2 how heavy he was
   3 how valuable he was
   4 how large he was
      A 1 and 2 only
      B 1 and 4 only
      C 2 and 3 only
      D 2 and 4 only

B   The Tea Shop

   A bus took him to the West End, where, among the crazy-
   coloured fountains of illumination, shattering the blue dusk
   with green and crimson fire, he found the café of his choice,
   a tea shop that had gone mad and turned Babylonian, a
5 white palace with ten thousand lights. It towered above the

37

older buildings like a citadel, which indeed it was, the outpost of a new age, perhaps a new civilisation, perhaps a new barbarism, and behind the thin marble front were concrete and steel, just as behind the careless profusion of luxury were
10 millions of pence balanced to the last half-penny. Somewhere in the background, hidden away, behind the ten thousand lights and acres of white napery and bewildering, glittering rows of teapots, behind the thousand waitresses and cash-box girls and black-coated floor managers and temperamental
15 long-haired violinists, behind the mounds of shimmering bon-bons and multi-coloured Viennese pastries, the cauldrons of stewed steak, the vanloads of harlequin ices, were a few men who went to work juggling with fractions of a farthing, who knew how many units of electricity it took to finish a
20 steak-and-kidney pudding and how many minutes and seconds a waitress (five-foot-four in height and in average health) would need to carry a tray of given weight from the kitchen lift to the table in the far corner. In short, there was a warm, sensuous vulgar life flowering in the upper storeys and
25 cold science working in the basement. Such was the gigantic tea shop into which Turgis marched, in search not of mere refreshment but of all the enchantment of unfamiliar luxury. Perhaps he knew in his heart that men have conquered half the known world, looted whole kingdoms, and never arrived
30 at such luxury.

The place was built for him.

It was built for a great many other people too, and as usual they were all there. It steamed with humanity. The marble entrance-hall, piled dizzily with bonbons and cakes, was as
35 crowded and bustling as a railway station. The gloom and grime of the streets, the raw air, all November, were at once left behind, forgotten: the atmosphere inside was golden, tropical, belonging to some high midsummer of confectionery. Disdaining the lifts, Turgis, once more excited by the sight,
40 sound and smell of it all, climbed the wide staircase until he reached his favourite floor, where an orchestra led by a young Jewish violinist with wandering, lustrous eyes and a passion for tremolo effects, acted as a magnet to a thousand girls. The door was swung open to him by a page; there burst, like a
45 sugary bomb, the clatter of cups, the shrill chatter of white-and-vermilion girls, and, cleaving the golden-scented air, the sensuous clamour of the strings; and, as he stood hesitat-

ing a moment, half dazed, there came bowing, a sleek grave
man, older than he was, and far more distinguished than he
50 could ever hope to be, who murmured deferentially: "For one,
sir? This way, please." Shyly yet proudly Turgis followed him.

That was the snag really, though. This place was so crowded
that you had to take the seat they offered you; there was no
picking and choosing your company at the table. And, as
55 usual, Turgis was not lucky. The vacant seat which he was
shown, and which he dare not refuse, was at a table already
occupied by three people, and not one of them remotely
resembled a nice-looking girl. There were two stout middle-
aged women, voluble, perspiring, and happy over cream
60 buns, and a middle-aged man who, no doubt, had been of no
great size even before this expedition started, but was now
very small and huddled, and gave the impression that if the
party stayed there much longer he would shrink to nothing
but spectacles, a nose, a collar and a pair of boots. For the
65 first few minutes Turgis was so disappointed that he was quite
angry with these people, hated them. And of course it was
impossible to get hold of a waitress. After five minutes or so
of glaring and waiting, he began to wish he had gone somewhere else. There was a pretty girl at the next table, but she
70 was obviously with her young man, and so fond of him that
every now and then she clutched his arm and held it tight,
just as if the young man might be thinking of running away.
At another table, not far way, were three girls together, two
of whom looked very interesting, with saucy eyes and wide
75 smiling mouths, but they were too busy whispering and
giggling to take any notice of him. So Turgis suddenly
stopped being a bright youth shooting amorous glances, and
became a stern youth who wanted some tea, who had gone
there for no other purpose than to obtain some tea, who was
80 surprised and indignant because no tea was forthcoming.

from *Angel Pavement* by JB Priestley

1 "fountains of illumination" (line 2) are best described as
 A watery lights
 B lights which play over fountains
 C sudden perceptions
 D spurting sources of light

2 A "citadel" (line 6) is best defined as
   A a fortress
   B a towering building
   C a safe place
   D a new building

3 The author's description of the "new age" as "perhaps a new civilisation, perhaps a new barbarism" (lines 7-8) suggests that he
   A wholly approves of it
   B wholly disapproves of it
   C does not take it seriously
   D finds it frightening

4 The author compares the concrete and steel of the structure of the tea shop (line 8) with
   A a palace
   B an Eastern building
   C the control of finances behind the enterprise
   D the appearance of luxury

5 The main point made in lines 10-23 is that
   A everything in the tea shop is controlled by the need to make a profit
   B there are far more people working in the building than is really necessary
   C the rooms are more pleasant as you get higher in the building
   D no one knows how such a place is organized

6 In the first paragraph the author emphasizes all the following aspects of the tea shop EXCEPT
   A the great quantities of food
   B the many different sorts of people working there
   C the care with which the whole place is organized
   D the large numbers of customers in the building

7 We are told towards the end of the first paragraph that Turgis went into the tea shop because
   A he needed a cup of tea
   B he could not understand how the place was run
   C he wanted the sort of comfort he did not usually have
   D he wanted to meet a nice girl

8 The author compares the entrance hall of the tea shop with a

"railway station" (line 35) because
A both places are likely to be full of people
B the entrance hall leads on to the tea room just as the railway station leads on to the trains
C both places would be full of steam
D both places would be very noisy

9 "Disdaining" (line 39) is nearest in meaning to
A avoiding
B ignoring
C scorning
D disliking

10 The author ascribes all the following qualities to the "Jewish violinist" (line 42) EXCEPT
A shining eyes
B poor playing
C sex appeal
D emotional, quivering sounds

11 As the door to the tea room was opened for him, Turgis noticed (line 44) all the following sounds EXCEPT
A the sound of violins
B people talking
C the noise of cups against saucers
D people clamouring to be served

12 Which **two** qualities of the noise are suggested by describing the sound of the tea room as "a sugary bomb" (line 45)? The comparison suggests
    1 destructiveness
    2 suddenness
    3 attractiveness
    4 fearfulness
    A 1 and 3 only
    B 1 and 4 only
    C 2 and 3 only
    D 2 and 4 only

13 "deferentially"(line 50) is nearest in meaning to
A gratefully
B respectfully
C patiently
D quietly

14 As Turgis followed the waiter into the tea room he felt
   A a pleasurable confusion of feelings
   B no feelings at all
   C in a state of extreme conflict of feeling
   D a painful tension between what he felt and how he appeared

15 The first few sentences of the last paragraph are different in style from the rest of the passage in order to
   A convey the feelings that Turgis had
   B convey the thoughts that he might have uttered
   C show up the inadequacy of the tea room
   D provide a change for the reader

16 For what **two reasons** was Turgis annoyed in the last paragraph? He was annoyed because
   1 there was far too much noise in the tea room
   2 he was not allowed to choose who he was going to sit near
   3 he thought the behaviour of people at nearby tables to be improper
   4 the people at his own table were eating creams buns
   5 he could not get served
      A 1 and 2 only
      B 1 and 4 only
      C 2 and 3 only
      D 2 and 5 only
      E 4 and 5 only

17 At the table where Turgis was seated there were
   A a nice-looking girl, two women and a man
   B a vacant seat, two women and a nice-looking girl
   C two stout women and a middle-aged man
   D a vacant seat and a middle-aged man

18 When Turgis noticed that two of the girls on a nearby table "looked very interesting" (line 74), he was probably thinking of
   A the sort of jobs they did
   B how attractive they looked
   C how well they would be able to discuss things
   D the interest they were showing in him

19 "shooting amorous glances" (line 77) is best explained as
   A trying to attract the waitress's eye

B looking about the room in a random fashion
C staring back at people looking at him
D looking provocatively at girls he found attractive

20 At the end of the passage Turgis changed his mood. This was, above all, because
A there were no attractive girls in the tea room
B he was tired of waiting
C the attractive girls were not taking any notice of him
D he disliked being ignored by waitresses

C Sunday Morning Life on the Common

Sunday morning on the Common has a distinction of its own. The people who live on the Common are wealthy. They need high-powered cars to reach their otherwise inaccessible homes and they need high-powered homes to make the
5 journey worthwhile. Like a class in school, they are all much the same age, wear the same sort of clothes and specialise, with only slightly varying degrees of success, in the subject of money. Every week contains at least two clear days of leisure, but on Sunday they rest. Sunday is a recurrent observance
10 that has nothing to do with God, and yet contains in its pro-longed silences, the distant pealing of bells, the wafts of roast mutton across the undisturbed bracken, the lazy spirals of smoke, a nostalgic piety; a sense, as in remembering old Sundays and old summers, of lassitude and loss.

15 Except for the occasional lonely child, too young to be sent to school, no one stirs until midday. The mutton is roasted and the apple pies are prepared by capable cooks, German or Swiss or Norwegian, who are saving up enough money to travel round the world. Later in the day they will mount their
20 bicycles and pedal in organised groups to each other's houses where they will eat tinned frankfurters and potato salad, smoke Turkish cigarettes and discuss the advantages of India over Brazil. Most of them call their employers by their Christian names and spend much of the day in a state of slight
25 and agreeable intoxication owing to the glasses of sherry continually pressed on them to keep them happy.

At noon, all over the Common, like a series of elaborate cuckoo-clocks, the various front doors open and the stock-brokers and dentists, company directors and chartered
30 accountants, directors of advertising agencies and manu-

facturers of plastic, step out on to their baize-green grass and reverently breathe the Sunday air. The literary agent, the film director and the playwright, their tenure less secure, emerge a few minutes later, hurriedly and guiltily inspecting
35 the gravel for weeds while nobody is looking. High yew hedges, roosters and domes of privet, sometimes an acre of wild land, separate these houses from each other, and yet an aerial view would show a solitary figure in each garden, the same flash of doggy yellow or hunting pink, the same white flag
40 of newspaper carelessly folded after breakfast; and, in a little while, the same tiny wives, popping out like an afterthought into the sun.

The wives have less resemblance to each other than the men. They conform to a certain standard of dress, they run their
45 houses along the same lines, bring their children up in the same way; all prefer coffee to tea, all drive cars, play bridge, own at least one valuable piece of jewellery and are moderately good-looking. That is all that can be seen. But it isn't all.

The relationships between the men are based on an under-
50 standing of success. Admiration is general, affection not uncommon. Even pity is known. The women have no such understanding. Like little icebergs, each keeps a bright and shining face above water; below the surface, submerged in fathoms of leisure, each keeps her own isolated personality.
55 Some are happy, some poisoned with boredom; some drink too much and some, below the demarcation line, are slightly crazy; some love their husbands and some are dying from lack of love; some have talent, as useless to them as a paralysed limb. Their friendships, appearing frank and sunny, are
60 febrile and short-lived, turning quickly to malice. Combined, their energy could start a revolution, power half of Southern England, drive an atomic plant. It is all directed towards the effortless task of living on the Common. There are times, towards the middle of the school term, when the quiet air
65 seems charged, ready to split lightning; when it is dangerous to touch a shrilling telephone and a coffee cup may explode without reason.

There is however, no sign of this as, dressed for Sunday in tight checked pants and cashmere sweaters, the wives join
70 their husbands in the bronze and gold September gardens. A few, the hosts for this morning, stay where they are. Some

44

take their dogs and set out slowly, couples meeting and
greeting on the winding, spongy paths, sometimes going on
together, sometimes parting. Those who live on the periphery
75 of the Common get out their cars and bowl like black, glinting
marbles along the unfenced roads. There is not one heretic;
not one Commoner who, on this mellow Sunday morning,
does not taste the sweet comfort of sherry, the content of a
cheese straw.

from *Daddy's Gone A-Hunting* by Penelope Mortimer

1 The phrase "a distinction of its own" (line 1) means that
   A every Sunday morning is different from other Sunday
     mornings
   B Sunday morning is more pleasant than other mornings
   C Sunday morning is different from the other mornings of the
     week
   D the other mornings of the week are very dull

2 "inaccessible" (line 3) is best defined as
   A impossible to reach
   B distant
   C worthless
   D inconvenient

3 "a recurrent observance" (line 9) implies that the people on
  the Common
   A look the same every Sunday
   B make sure they do the same things every Sunday
   C repeat themselves when not in church
   D see the same things every Sunday

4 We are told that on Sundays all the following are regularly
  experienced on the Common EXCEPT
   A the sound of church bells
   B smells of dinners being cooked
   C lack of sound
   D attendance at church

5 When the Common dweller feels "a nostalgic piety" (line 13),
  he feels
   A sad and reverent about the past
   B a desire to attend church

C the holiness of silence

D a reverence towards the countryside

6 "lassitude" in line 14 is most closely defined as
A past failures
B tiredness
C regret
D age

7 The reference to "the occasional lonely child, too young to be sent to school" (line 15) implies that
A children on the Common go to school every day
B Sunday Schools flourish here
C children here go to boarding schools
D not many of the couples living on the Common have children

8 "they" in line 19 refers to
A the men who live on the Common
B the few children who are at home
C visitors who are staying with the Commoners
D young foreigners employed as servants

9 From the evidence in the second paragraph it is clear that the "capable cooks" (line 17) are treated by their employers
A in a disrespectful way
B in a friendly and concerned way
C so badly that they need to drink to keep happy
D as old-fashioned servants

10 The comparison "like a series of elaborate cuckoo-clocks" (line 27) is very appropriate in its context because
A the owners of the houses all come out regularly at the same time
B all the house fronts look similar
C the houses are built carefully and elaborately
D the owners come out of their houses and call to each other

11 We are informed that all the following types of people live on the Common EXCEPT
A literary agents
B writers
C chartered accountants
D clergymen

12 "The literary agent, the film director and the playwright" (line 32) are distinguished from the other dwellers on the Common because
A they feel themselves to be less successful
B they are more interested in gardening
C they look after their houses better
D they have more sensitive feelings

13 In the third paragraph, we are invited to look at the Common from **two** distinctively different angles. These different views are
  1 of the front doors of the houses
  2 from inside the houses
  3 of the land between the houses
  4 from above looking down into the gardens
    A 1 and 4 only
    B 2 and 3 only
    C 1 and 3 only
    D 2 and 4 only

14 From the evidence of the third paragraph, it is clear that the men spend part of Sunday mornings before noon
A weeding their drives
B hurrying out to visit each other
C reading the paper in the back garden
D going hunting

15 "conform to a certain standard of dress" (line 44) most closely implies that
A the wives do not worry much about how they dress
B they all agree to dress very well
C they share the same ideas about the appropriate way to dress
D they all dress boringly

16 Which of the following best summarizes the content of the fifth paragraph?
A The men can understand each other's needs but all the women tend to drink too much and fail to use their talents. They are too energetic which causes them to have rows.
B Whereas the men do understand each other, the women are isolated from each other and frustrated. They have more energy than their way of life on the Common requires and so become very tense.

C The women are less intelligent than the men and although they are happy, they are often bored and become malicious with each other instead of developing their friendships.

D Craziness, lack of love and too much drink cause the women to waste their lives. This could cause a revolution but life here is too effortless for them to want to change it.

17 In line 65 we are told that "it is dangerous to touch a shrilling telephone" because

A thunder-storms create electrical disturbances in the middle of the summer

B any movement may precipitate a row with one of the women

C they may hear bad news about their children at school

D someone may be listening in to the conversation

18 In the final paragraph those who "stay where they are" (line 71) are

A the people who are giving the drinks parties

B the people who prefer to sit in their gardens than to visit the others

C the children who are not at school

D the foreign cooks who are preparing lunch

19 "like black, glinting marbles" (line 75) is an appropriate comparison for the cars for which **two** of the following reasons? It is appropriate because

1 the cars run smoothly so that you can hardly hear their engines

2 marbles are small dashing things like the cars

3 the cars are very highly powered and can go fast

4 the cars are highly polished and gleaming

A 1 and 2 only

B 3 and 4 only

C 1 and 3 only

D 1 and 4 only

20 "heretic" in line 76 may best be defined as some one who

A disbelieves in Christianity

B is discontented and irritable

C prefers to be alone rather than to mix with others

D does not hold the opinions or participate in the activities of others around him

48

Chapter 4
Understanding Information and Argument

The passages in this chapter contain factual information rather than feelings and imagined responses. They contain ideas and arguments and very often the author introduces information, facts and figures, simply in order to support an assertion, to drive home his argument. Sometimes this sort of writing can be difficult to understand: there seem to be so many details to take into account, so many twists and turns to the argument. Do not despair! Take the passage paragraph by paragraph and try to come to terms with each one as you read it through. Ask yourself what main point the author is making in each paragraph. Do not try to digest the whole passage in one swallow: chew over each bit separately. Many of the questions that follow the passages will, in fact, help you to do this.

A   The Trade Unions and Industrial Change

We have seen earlier how the textile workers at the beginning of the nineteenth century reacted to the threat of mechanisation by smashing the machines they feared. Today 'Luddism' could easily be prevented and punished. But some unions
5   operate a system which has been called 'neo-Luddism' or new Luddism, which simply means that if they do not want a particular process to be made automatic they will threaten the employers with a strike. Sometimes a very powerful union has succeeded in compelling a company to agree to
10   paying men for work that they no longer do, before they would allow a new machine to be introduced. A famous example comes from the United States of America, where the Railway Brotherhood compelled the railway companies to maintain a crew of two to drive a diesel engine which
15   needed only one. The old steam engines had required a driver and a fireman, and the union did not want all the firemen to be thrown out of work.

One must sympathise with the situation of a man who has acquired a skill and who, late in life, is threatened with
20   unemployment and no prospect of being able to use his skill again to earn a living. We have also to remember that the prosperity of every country in the world depends upon its ability to keep abreast of technical progress. In Britain, we

have seen a number of industries decline in the last thirty or
25 forty years: coal, because of the competition of oil and
electricity; cotton and wool textiles, because of the invention
of rayon and other man-made fibres like nylon; railways,
because of road transport and airlines; shipbuilding, partly
because of air transport, and partly because so many countries
30 which used to buy British ships now build their own. International competition is naturally now much greater than in
the 'golden age' of Queen Victoria, when British manufacturers held the centre of the world stage.

The past experiences of skilled workers have made them
35 wary of change. Too often they have felt the cold and bitter
wind of change blowing away their livelihood, and bringing
them little or nothing in return. An ill wind, indeed, against
the blasts of which the trade unions are now expected to
protect them. If change is to take place in industry today,
40 then it must be with the full co-operation and consent of the
unions.

Because of the rapid advances in techniques made in certain
industries, trade unions sometimes find themselves overtaken
by events, and their immediate reaction tends to be defensive.
45 This is often the reason for 'demarcation disputes', where two
trade unions quarrel about which skilled worker is to do which
skilled job. If an engineering worker has to use wood and
metal together, he may find that the carpenters are demand-
ing that all the work on the wooden part should be done by
50 them. This slows down the work and requires more men to be
involved, and it all adds to the cost of the finished product.
The unions argue that their duty is towards their members,
not to the company nor to the country. This is understand-
able, when the history of trade-union struggles is considered,
55 but is still rather an old-fashioned view.

Sometimes, as in the printing industry, the resistance of the
trade unions to new methods makes the cost of production so
high that some companies find it impossible to continue in
business and have to close down. This hastens the decline of
60 an industry and puts members of the union out of work,
precisely the result that the union's policy was designed to
avoid.

We hear a great deal nowadays about a sweeping technical

revolution called automation. This very advanced form of
65 mechanisation, which will mean eventually that complete
factories can be operated by a handful of key workers and a
computer, will be the greatest labour-saver in history, and
will mean the disappearance of very many jobs. Because it is
likely to happen first in new industries like motor-car manu-
70 facture and electronics, the trade unions are not in a good
position to prevent it or delay it, because they are not so
well organised there as they are in the older industries. But
one of the vital tasks facing the trade unions today, precisely
because of the inevitable progress, is to bring themselves and
75 their organisation up to date, and to encourage their members
to accept new ideas and changes.

from *The Trade Unions* by Andrew Robertson

1 "Luddism" in line 3 may best be defined as
  A the workforce destroying machines being introduced into
    an industry
  B co-operation with industrial change
  C a union calling a strike because of inadequate wages
  D a union compelling a company to pay men for work they
    no longer do

2 The main idea presented in the first paragraph is that
  A Luddism could easily be prevented
  B men should not be paid less when new machines are
    introduced
  C strikes are now used by unions as a means of stopping the
    introduction of new machines
  D examples of Luddism now come from the USA

3 In the first paragraph the Railway Brotherhood is cited as an
  example of a union that
  A promoted more efficiency in its industry
  B successfully opposed the introduction of new machinery
  C forced its company to take on extra men where they were
    not necessary
  D forced its companies to maintain the same level of employ-
    ment despite the introduction of new machinery

4 The main argument the author wishes to imply in the second
  paragraph is

A no man who has acquired a skill should be forced out of work
B Britain must, at all costs, maintain technical and industrial growth
C too many industries in Britain are declining
D many countries who used to buy British goods now manufacture their own

5 In lines 23–30, the author asserts that all the following industries have declined EXCEPT
A shipbuilding
B coal
C man-made fibres
D railways

6 The author thinks shipbuilding (line 28) has declined for which **two** of the following reasons? It has declined because
  1 of the development of air transport
  2 there is less need for exporting and importing
  3 other countries no longer buy British ships
  4 international competition has increased
    A 1 and 2 only
    B 2 and 3 only
    C 1 and 3 only
    D 3 and 4 only

7 The statement, "British manufacturers held the centre of the world stage" (line 32) implies that
A British goods looked better than they were
B British manufacturers advertized their products in a theatrical way
C British products were so good that no one thought of challenging their pre-eminent position
D the British industrialists were constantly showing off to the rest of the world

8 In line 35, the phrase "wary of change" implies that
A skilled workers are aware of the importance of change
B they fear change
C they have many memories of change
D they are weary of having to adapt

9 The author says that the essential condition for change in industry (line 39) is

A the wariness of the workers
B adequate returns in the form of wages for workers
C that the unions should protect their members
D the unions' agreement to allow change

10 "techniques" (line 42) is best defined as
A machinery
B ways of doing things
C automation
D changing procedures

11 Which one of the following words is closest in meaning to "defensive" (line 44)?
A timid
B guarded
C swift
D self-protective

12 The author implies that the main conflict in any "demarcation dispute" (line 45) is
A between individual workers
B between management and the unions
C between a union and its members
D between one union and another

13 In the fourth paragraph, the author identifies all the following reasons against retaining absolute lines of demarcation in jobs EXCEPT
A slowing down of the work
B poorer quality of the product
C need for more workers to be involved
D increased cost of the product

14 "This" in line 50 refers to
A the history of trade union struggles
B demarcation disputes
C the attitude of the unions
D the rising costs of labour

15 The "printing industry" (line 56) is mentioned as an example of an industry where
A business failure has resulted from union action
B new methods have proved too expensive
C unions have co-operated with management
D management has been unsympathetic to union views

16 Which **two** results does the author believe will follow automation? It will result in
    1 far more efficient industrial action
    2 loss of many jobs
    3 saving of much labour
    4 cheaper goods on the market
    A 1 and 2 only
    B 2 and 3 only
    C 2 and 4 only
    D 3 and 4 only

17 "electronics" (line 70) is quoted because it is
    A similar to motor-car manufacture
    B a badly organized industry
    C a recently established industry
    D keen to introduce automation

18 "it" in line 71 refers to
    A new industry
    B automation
    C loss of many jobs
    D the computer

19 The word "inevitable" (line 74) could best be replaced by
    A amazing
    B unavoidable
    C predictable
    D rapid

20 From your understanding of the whole passage, do you think that the author is primarily arguing that
    A British industry must look for new markets
    B management should be more aware of the problems of workers
    C unions should have less power over their members
    D unions should be more prepared to allow for change

B Television Reporting and Newspaper Reporting

The practical arguments for the supremacy of the printed word over the television interview are at least as strong as the theoretical. Making the change from television to newspaper work, I have been struck by how much less easy it is for a television reporter to find out what has happened or is happening than it is for a newspaper reporter.

It is not simply that I can get about better now: that I am one instead of at least three, that I have no camera crew with me whose movements I delay and who delay mine, that the luggage with me need consist only of a suitcase and a typewriter instead of more than a dozen bulky boxes. It is not even that getting a story into a newspaper is so much less arduous a business than getting a piece of television on to the air: a typewriter and a telephone replace the whole rigmarole of aeroplane and satellite and film labs and viewing theatres and editing machines, with the result that the reporter has much more time to work in before the material need leave his hand. What counts is the psychological difference between a camera, or any recording device, and a notebook. You notice it as soon as you sit down with someone who can tell you what you want to know. If there is a camera behind you, your man is aware that he is not really talking to you at all. He is talking to anyone who might be listening, total strangers, his family, his employers, his voters. His words are guarded, self-conscious. It is the same if there is a microphone in front of him, and two rotating rolls of magnetic tape slowly recording the sound for radio.

It is not the same if the only piece of recording equipment produced is a notebook. Even if he is self-conscious at first, your informant quickly sees that not everything he says is written down. There will be gaps – there may be long gaps – between the interesting or important things he says; and in consequence there will be long periods while the notebook is unused, and he rapidly forgets so apparently innocuous a device in his admirable anxiety that you should see the affair in hand as he does.

There are many occasions when a newspaper reporter need not use a notebook at all until after the talk is over. Storing the mind with things said, like a chipmunk filling its cheeks with maize, and then disgorging them on to the pages of a notebook, is a technique comparatively easily learnt. It has the advantage that it makes not merely the answers flow more readily but the questions too, since the reporter is not half-

preoccupied with writing down the answer to one question
45 while he devises the next. It can only be used if the results of
the interview are either not going to be quoted at all or
quoted anonymously, since for attributed quotation it is not
precise enough. But those are often the most interesting quotations —too revealing, or too damaging, to be fathered on their
50 originator without his express permission: the borough
architect's reflection on his council's collective taste, the
backbencher's unease about the party leadership.

Television reporters hear that kind of observation at least
as often as newspaper reporters – perhaps more often, in
55 moments of post-interview relaxation, when the subject is
relieved and a little surprised at having guarded himself so
well from indiscretion. But television reporters cannot use it.
They have to use the interview instead, the discreet bromide.

from *Journalism and Government* by John Whale

1 The main point of the first paragraph is that
   A theoretical arguments are part of newspaper reporting
   B it is easier to be a television reporter than it is to be a
      newspaper reporter
   C the printed word is more important than television
   D it is easier to work as a newspaper reporter than as a
      television reporter

2 In the second paragraph, the author says that the main problem
  for the television interviewer is
   A getting the camera crew to the scene of the interview
   B needing the time for transmitting and editing the film
   C that the man being interviewed is more guarded and self-
      conscious
   D that the man being interviewed talks to other people

3 The subject of the third paragraph is
   A how easily people forget they are being interviewed
   B the lack of interesting things people say in interviews
   C that people being interviewed want you to see things from
      their point of view
   D that using only a notebook helps the person being inter-
      viewed to be less self-conscious

4 In the fourth paragraph, the author is discussing
   A the advantages and disadvantages of not using a notebook
   B the difficulty of quoting revealing or damaging statements
   C the ease of running an interview if you do without a note-
      book
   D how easy it is to remember a whole interview

5 The most important point in the final paragraph is that
   A the subject is more off-guard after a television interview
   B television reporters cannot make use of off-guard state-
      ments
   C television reporters hear more interesting observations
      than newspaper reporters
   D people being interviewed are surprised at how well they
      can guard themselves from indiscretion

6 "supremacy" (line 1) is nearest in meaning to
   A power
   B greatness
   C higher authority
   D clarity

7 In this context, "the printed word" (line 1) refers to
   A a television script
   B what a reporter writes in his notebook
   C published books
   D news conveyed through printed reports

8 The writer says he can get about better now (line 7) for all the
   following reasons EXCEPT
   A he is on his own
   B he is fitter than he used to be
   C he has no camera crew with him
   D he has no bulky baggage

9 "arduous" (line 13) is nearest in meaning to
   A steep
   B laborious
   C lengthy
   D exhausting

10 When the author uses the word "rigmarole" (line 14), he is
   regarding the preparation of a television report
   A seriously

B   despairingly
C   humorously
D   knowingly

11 All of the following are necessary in the preparation of a
   television report EXCEPT
   A   aeroplanes
   B   telephones
   C   film labs
   D   editing machines

12 The man being interviewed by a television reporter is likely
   to be all of the following EXCEPT
   A   self-conscious in front of the camera
   B   worried about his family or his employers
   C   really talking to the interviewer
   D   really thinking about his voters

13 In line 26, the author suggests that the effect of a microphone
   is the same as that of
   A   a television camera
   B   a newspaper reporter
   C   a television reporter
   D   a tape recorder

14 "apparently innocuous" (line 34) means
   A   harmless in appearance
   B   really deceitful
   C   dangerous in appearance
   D   obviously useless

15 The reporter will not use his notebook for long periods (line 33)
   because
   A   he wants the subject to feel at ease
   B   the subject is saying nothing interesting or important in
       those periods
   C   he forgets this innocuous device
   D   he is recording the interview on tape

16 "in hand" (line 36) means
   A   in the balance
   B   under control
   C   being considered
   D   exactly

17 The word "admirable" (line 35) suggests all the following feelings on the part of the author EXCEPT
   A praise
   B approval
   C patronage
   D scorn

18 "like a chipmunk" (line 39) is an effective simile because it relates to an animal which
   A has capacious cheeks
   B can run fast
   C can eat effectively
   D can store things for later use

19 The word closest in meaning to "anonymously" (line 47) is
   A namelessly
   B briefly
   C impressively
   D secretly

20 The reporter who does not use a notebook cannot quote what his subject says because
   A it would be too damaging to the subject
   B it would result in legal action
   C he cannot be sure of the exact words spoken by his subject
   D he does not have the subject's permission to quote them

21 "fathered on" (line 49) suggests
   A looked after by
   B attributed to
   C moved beyond
   D reproduced by

22 The "borough architect" (line 50) is mentioned because
   A he may be a typical subject to be interviewed
   B he is obviously indiscreet
   C he has bad taste
   D he is likely to have difficulties with his council

23 "that kind of observation" (line 53) refers to
   A political comments
   B close-ups on television
   C unguarded indiscretions
   D viewing with consideration

24 In the final paragraph we are told that after an interview, a
   subject tends to feel
   A more relaxed and ready to talk
   B shocked by his own indiscretion
   C unwilling to say any more
   D keen to guard himself from indiscretion

25 "Television reporters cannot use" (line 57)
   A chemicals other than bromide
   B surprised comments during the interview
   C revealing quotations
   D indiscretions made after the interview

C The Case For and Against Small Primary Schools

In education, the main theme in rural areas has been reorganisation and consolidation into fewer, larger schools.
Primary schools have suffered greatly in this process. In the
former East Riding, the number of primary schools dropped
5 from 235 in 1946 to 151 in 1970, a decrease of 36% in 24 years.
The impetus underlying this movement has been part
educational and part economic, with the sceptics laying stress
upon the latter. Labour represents a proportionately larger
cost in small schools and the minimum 'economic' size is
10 probably a one-form entry school with roughly 210 pupils. Of
late, the pace has slackened as the extra costs of transporting
children has outstripped the savings made by school closures.
There has also been a major report, Gittins on Primary
Education in Wales (1967), which proposed a minimum size
15 for primary schools of 60 pupils (say, three teachers) but even
this has provoked opposition from defenders of smaller
schools. Many schools are still well below the Gittins lower
limits and, in practice, it seems that only those with fewer
than 40 pupils are in danger of 'reorganisation'.

20 The educational arguments against small rural schools take
their cue directly from the modern world. At the upper end
of the primary school, the curriculum has expanded so
rapidly, to cover subjects such as French, Science, and
Music, that there are now too many and diverse interests for
25 one or two teachers to cover adequately, and children in
small schools could be disadvantaged by the limited range
offered to them. Very similar arguments apply to equipment
and materials. Economics apart, it may be physically im-

possible to house all the equipment considered essential for
30 modern education in a small, out-dated building. Activity
spaces, music rooms, television, film projectors and cookery
bays, are all extensive in their use of space – which is at a
premium in small schools.

The arguments have a psychological and social slant as well.
35 Psychology stresses the dangers inherent in a small school
where the dominance of one teacher may be unrelieved;
the school could thrive under the influence of a good teacher
but equally it may suffer under a mediocre one. Sociology
refers to the influx of people from the town into country areas
40 and their demands for urban standards of education which, it
is said, are superior and cannot be met within the limitations
of a small school.

The proponents of the small school are not without arguments
of their own to stress. There are advantages derived from
45 small, vertically grouped classes where children of different
ages help each other, the older children gaining particularly
in terms of responsibility and self-expression. The value of
this traditional teaching method has been demonstrated by
its adoption in larger, urban schools. Young children also
50 benefit from the confidence and security obtained from
smaller groups and from the individual attention allowed by
a low pupil–staff ratio and low staff turnover. Discipline is
rarely a problem and the vitally important links between
home and school can be strong, a point which readily merges
55 with a more general one, namely the social advantages that
can be gained by the use of the school as a focal point for
community life. With the expanding horizons of the modern
world, a demand for a variety of interests could be met by
peripatetic teachers serving a group of village schools (and
60 cheaply too; the costs of transporting one person are less than
those of transporting an entire school), whilst the educational
administrator may prefer smaller units for the flexibility they
give in meeting unforeseen population changes and the
grouping of children into secondary school catchment areas.

from *Rural Planning Problems* edited by Gordon E Cherry

1 "This movement" (line 6) may be most precisely defined as
  A the transportation of children to school
  B the reduction in the number of schools in the East Riding

C the reorganization of schools in country areas

D the merging of small rural primary schools into fewer larger ones

2 "sceptics" (line 7) are people who

A disbelieve in high-minded motives

B believe in saving money

C want to provide the best possible educational system

D think that economic motivations are always the most powerful

3 The statement, "Labour represents a proportionately larger cost in small schools", means

A teachers in small schools earn more than they would in larger schools

B it is necessary to employ more teachers in a number of small schools than in fewer larger schools

C it is harder work teaching in smaller schools than in larger ones

D the Labour Party disapproves of the high cost of small schools

4 What **two** reasons are offered in paragraph one for the drop in numbers of primary schools? The reasons are

1 there has been a reduction in the birthrate

2 the Gittins Report advised fewer, larger primary schools

3 it is cheaper to staff fewer larger schools than more smaller ones

4 it is cheaper to transport children than to maintain small local schools

5 money saved from closures can be used to employ more teachers

A 1 and 5 only

B 1 and 3 only

C 2 and 3 only

D 3 and 4 only

E 3 and 5 only

5 In line 18, the author uses the phrase "in practice" to imply that

A the authorities will not rigorously apply the policy stated in the Gittins report

B small schools are used to policies of reorganization

C small schools have to work very hard to maintain their standards

D small schools will be reorganized, as the Gittins report advocated

6 "the pace" (line 11) refers to
   A the rate at which teachers are given rises in salary
   B the rate at which small schools are closed and larger ones formed
   C the speed of transporting children to school
   D the rate at which costs of transporting children to school have risen

7 "the curriculum" (line 22) is best defined as
   A modern demands
   B arts subjects
   C content of lessons
   D subjects taught in schools

8 The phrase "Economics apart,"(line 28) may be most accurately restated as
   A leaving aside the question of cost
   B leaving out the subject, economics, from the teaching
   C part of the problem being economics
   D because economics is different

9 "disadvantaged" (line 26) means
   A lacking in ability
   B narrowly missing opportunities
   C unable to make progress
   D denied the benefits of something

10 In the second paragraph, which two arguments are put forward against small rural schools? The arguments are
     1 the range of subjects required to be taught cannot adequately be covered by the teachers
     2 it costs too much to equip small schools for all the subjects required
     3 the out-dated buildings of these schools need expensive renovation
     4 there is not sufficient room in the schools to house the necessary equipment
     A 1 and 2 only
     B 1 and 3 only

    C 1 and 4 only
    D 2 and 3 only
    E 2 and 4 only

11 "unrelieved" (line 36) may best be replaced by
    A tired
    B changeable
    C unsympathetic
    D unchanging

12 The author says that people who move from towns into
country areas (line 39) want
    A better schools than they had in the towns
    B the same level of education that is provided in the towns
    C smaller schools than in the towns
    D a superior education to what exists

13 Which **two** arguments are put forward in paragraph three
against small rural schools? The arguments are
    1 too many teachers are mediocre
    2 psychologists oppose them because they see the dangers
    3 too much depends on the ability of a single teacher
    4 people who have recently moved send their children back
       to the towns for school
    5 people recently moved from towns demand schools like
       those they have been used to
    A 1 and 3 only
    B 2 and 4 only
    C 3 and 5 only
    D 4 and 5 only

14 "Proponents" (line 43) are people who
    A oppose
    B criticize
    C argue against
    D justify

15 "vertically grouped classes" (line 45) are
    A classes with rows of desks
    B housed in tower blocks
    C classes of children of different ages
    D classes of children of the same age

16 "this traditional teaching method" (line 48) refers to

A the use of blackboards and chalk
B the use of older children to teach younger ones
C the way teaching is carried out in large urban schools
D the presence of one good teacher all the time

17 All the following reasons for keeping small rural schools
are included in the sentence that begins, "Discipline is
rarely . . ." (lines 52-57) EXCEPT that
A there are few problems over bad behaviour
B the home and the school can work closely together
C the teachers know all the pupils very well
D the school plays an important part in the local community

18 "Peripatetic" (line 59) means
A travelling
B inexpensive
C inefficient
D stimulating

19 The reason for the administrator's preference for small rural
schools would be that
A it is cheaper to run them
B they can always be grouped together into larger schools
C they allow for more possibilities when planning for the
future
D they can accommodate more children if the population
increases

20 From your reading of the whole passage, do you think the aim
of the author is primarily to
A present an unbiased account of the arguments for and
against small primary schools
B gain support for the existence of small schools
C try to encourage support for the changes taking place
D urge the creation of larger primary schools

D The Aims and Purposes of the Social Services
In the past, services provided by the community through
either voluntary or statutory organisations to relieve the poor
could justifiably be distinguished as social services, but so too
could services intended to maintain the living standards of
5 the community as a whole, for example, public-health
services, the police, public libraries, street lighting, roads,
and public parks. If, however, we wish to isolate the social

services as being different from other services socially or publicly provided, and it looks as though we do, then the
10 criterion of direct concern with personal well-being would seem to be an adequate method of differentiation. Thus poor relief is always given to individual persons, and so too are medical care, education, unemployment benefit, an old-age pension, and the like, whereas street lighting, public parks,
15 libraries, sanitation, water supplies, and similar services are made available generally. It could be argued therefore that the social services are those provided by the community for no other reason than that of maintaining or improving individual well-being.

20 "For no other reason" is essential and is intended to distinguish these services from those which have aims other than the individual well-being of the recipients of the service. For example, commercial and industrial services of various kinds are provided under a capitalist system so as to benefit not
25 only the recipients but also those who provide the service. There is the profit motive, and though in order to make a profit good quality services have (or ought) to be given to the recipients, there is obviously the initial motive of benefit to the person providing the service. This simple truth was
30 clearly recognised in the eighteenth century by the "father" of British economic theory, Adam Smith, when he wrote "Not from the benevolence of the butcher do we expect our dinner but from his regard for his own interest." We are not concerned with the ethics of the capitalist system, or the
35 effectiveness of the profit motive as a means of raising living standards, but merely to show that in providing social services there is no thought of direct profit. There is (or ought to be) no other reason than that of ensuring individual well-being.

40 In recent years, especially since the end of the Second World War, the impression has been created that the social services are no longer directed at the particular needs of individuals, and in part this is due to the introduction of the concept of the universality of welfare provisions. The turning point
45 marking the transfer of attention from the few to the many was probably the publication of the Beveridge Report in 1942. Hitherto the statutory social services had been limited to particular occupational and income groups, whereas the Beveridge proposals concerned all the adult population

50 irrespective of occupation or income. For example, National
   Insurance against interruption or cessation of income was not
   henceforth to be confined to low income or specified
   occupational groups, and a National Health service was to be
   made available to everyone from the cradle to the grave. The
55 emphasis on universality obscured the fact that even with
   these sweeping changes the benefits obtained were still
   limited to persons having specified needs in times of specified
   contingencies, and therefore the basic principle of ensuring
   individual well-being was (and still is) applicable.

60 The belief that the aims and purposes of the social services
   had been completely revolutionized by the introduction of
   the concept of universality was further strengthened by the
   passing of the Family Allowances Act, 1945. All parents
   having more than one child were to be given a standard
65 allowance for each child by the State. Did this therefore
   mean the abandonment of the principle of need as a criterion
   for the provision of a social service?

   Some would argue that it did, because even the wealthiest
   parents became entitled to family allowances, and of course
70 millionaires are just as entitled to National Health medical
   services as the (financially) poorest members of the community. However, wealthy parents do not in fact receive as
   much as the less wealthy because family allowances are
   subject to income tax; and millionaires need not necessarily
75 avail themselves of the service provided by the National
   Health Service. In any case is there any real difference
   between giving a family allowance to parents whose income
   from employment does not take into account family responsi-
   bilities and the child allowance granted as a relief under the
80 Finance Acts to income-taxpayers?

   There are by now infinite varieties of social provision which
   make the task of distinguishing the social services from other
   forms of social provision extremely difficult. There would
   seem to be no rational basis on which to make such dis-
85 tinctions, and Professor R. M. Titmuss has shown that the
   social divisions of welfare are far more complex and irrational
   than most people imagine. Yet many persist in believing that
   the social services are only for the poor or working classes
   (undefined) whose standards of living are raised by the gener-
90 osity of taxpayers whose incomes are compulsorily reduced

by the State so that the amounts taken by taxation can be redistributed among the recipients of the social services.

from *The Future of the Welfare State* by David C Marsh

1 "statutory" (line 2) may best be defined as
   A permanent
   B compulsory
   C established by law
   D officially recognized

2 The main distinction the author makes in the first sentence is between
   A services provided by the community and the services of voluntary organizations
   B services intended to relieve the poor and services intended for the benefit of the whole community
   C services concerned with health and services related to the maintenance of the environment
   D social services and public services

3 The word "distinguished" (line 3) may most appropriately be replaced by
   A characterized
   B honoured
   C considered adequate
   D noticed

4 In the first paragraph, the author sees all the following as social services maintaining the standard of life of the whole community EXCEPT
   A public parks
   B public libraries
   C the police force
   D unemployment benefit

5 In the first paragraph, the author distinguished the social services from other services publicly or socially provided by
   A defining them as poor relief
   B identifying them mainly with maintenance of living standards
   C relating them to individual well-being
   D relating them to the health of the community

6 "recipients" (line 22) are people who
   A receive
   B contribute
   C support
   D depend

7 "the butcher" (line 32) is included as an example of someone who
   A earns his own living by exploiting others
   B could also be found in the eighteenth century
   C provides services for others in order to benefit himself
   D provides services in which there is no thought of excessive profit

8 "This simple truth" (line 29) is that
   A commercial services are provided in order to make a profit
   B butchers are too concerned to make profits
   C in order to make a profit, good quality services must be provided
   D the capitalist system is unethical

9 The main point in lines 33-39 is that
   A commercial and industrial services are provided in order to make a profit for those who provide the services
   B the only acceptable definition of social services is services provided for the benefit of individuals
   C the profit motive is an effective way of raising living standards for everyone
   D there are important differences between services run to make a profit and those organized for the benefit of individuals

10 Since the Second World War the impression has been created that the social services are no longer directed at the needs of individuals (line 40). This impression has resulted from
   A the reduction in the supplementary income available for specified occupational groups
   B the inefficient organization of the social services
   C the abandonment of the principle of need as a criterion for the provision of a social service
   D the application of welfare provisions to all members of the community

11 The main proposal of the Beveridge Report (line 46) is,

according to the author, that

A social services should be limited to the poorer people

B all people should be able to benefit from the social services whatever their incomes

C National Insurance against loss of income should be compulsory for everyone

D a National Health Service should be available to everyone throughout their lives

12 The word "cessation" (line 51) may most appropriately be replaced by

A stoppage

B abandonment

C reduction

D lack

13 "specified contingencies" (line 57) may best be defined as

A previously defined occurrences

B particular hardships

C additional difficulties

D anticipated subsidiary aspects

14 "The emphasis on universality" (line 55) refers to

A Britain's efforts to be at peace in the world

B the attempt to make social services available for everyone

C the desire to raise living standards in Britain

D the desire to raise living standards throughout the world

15 The question that the author raises in connection with the Family Allowances Act, 1945 (line 63) is whether

A all parents having more than one child deserve the allowance for each child

B all parents should have the allowance whether or not they have more than one child

C social services were now to be provided for people whether they needed the help or not

D social services should be provided as a matter of principle

16 "millionaires" (line 70) are mentioned because

A there can be no justification for their benefitting from the National Health Service

B they need medical help as much as anyone

C they do not, in fact, receive as much Family Allowance as poorer parents

    D they are to be included amongst those who have the right
       to receive National Health benefits

17 In the fifth paragraph, we are told that wealthy parents do not
    receive as much Family Allowance as the less wealthy because
    A they are not allowed to claim
    B they choose not to claim the allowance
    C they have to pay tax on the allowance
    D they have more family responsibilities

18 In lines 76-80 the author questions the difference between
    two similar situations. These two situations are
      1 parents paying less income-tax because they have children
         dependent on them
      2 parents earning more from employment than those who
         have no children
      3 parents receiving family allowance and gaining income-tax
         relief
      4 parents receiving family allowance but no tax relief for
         family responsibilities
      A 1 and 2 only
      B 2 and 3 only
      C 1 and 4 only
      D 3 and 4 only

19 The author asserts that it is difficult to distinguish social
    services from other forms of social provision (line 82) because
    A they all provide much the same help
    B there is no rationality behind their existence
    C welfare is applied to all classes of people
    D there are so many ways of helping people

20 The main point of the final sentence is that
    A people wrongly think that the poor are supported by taxes
       paid by the better off
    B the poor are in fact helped indirectly by the wealthy
    C the State forces the rich to pay taxes
    D people are wrong to think that the working classes need a
       higher standard of living

Answers

An asterisk (*) beside a letter indicates the correct answer.

Chapter 2

A   Toby Goes Exploring

1 Although the nun implied that Toby was a young boy, he is hardly likely to have had the complex thoughts and self-understanding in the first paragraph below the age of adolescence. On the other hand, the nun's reference to young boys would be wholly inappropriate if he were older than 18. C* seems the most likely answer.

2 There is a private cemetery (C) *within* the enclosure but that is not the whole of it. D is utterly fanciful though if you were confused you might have chosen it in desperation. It is possible that Toby might have been under the illusion that B was the case but the actual presence of the nuns means that A* is correct.

3 This question requires you to consider everything the nun does in Toby's presence. Toby might actually have felt rejected and patronized but it is clear that the nun was friendly from her first remark and tried to help him feel at ease whilst, at the same time, steering him firmly out of the grounds, as D* implies.

4 There is no evidence for A and the answers C and D could only arise from misreading the first paragraph. Toby knew that "sooner or later he *must* jump" (line 6) and that is the clue that should make you opt for B*.

5 "Agitated" means literally "moved" or "shaken" but since the whole focus of this paragraph is on Toby's feelings, A* is clearly more appropriate than B. There is no evidence for C and, as the answer to the previous question showed, Toby knew very well what he was going to do.

6 This question must be answered by looking closely at the context in which the phrase is used. There is no evidence for

A or B and C, even if true, refers far too widely and generally to be of use here. The answer must be D*.

7 The layout of the question may at first seem confusing but the heart of the answer is to be found by examining lines 20–22 of the passage. Toby imagines two possibilities: 2 and 3. These reflect his uncertainty as to whether he will be a source of terror or of delight to the nuns. C* is, therefore, the answer.

8 We are told in lines 22–24 that Toby felt alarm as a result of the pictures in his imagination. These imaginings are also "delicious" and so we may assume they gave him pleasure. He was "amazed", that is, surprised at this conflict of feelings. 1, 2 and 5 must, therefore, constitute the answer B*.

9 The definition which is closest to the meaning of "un-nerving" is D*. The word literally means taking away nerve or strength.

10 A* is the only possible implication of the statement. B, C and D introduce irrelevant elements that are not even hinted at in the passage. There is no evidence that the door is strong or intricate or that Toby wanted to smash it in.

11 The sentence that follows, on line 32, gives us the clue here. Toby was primarily aware of how far he would have to run back to escape over the enclosure wall. So C* must be the answer.

12 Toby hears A and C and we are told how much "the noise alarmed him" but we learn nothing about D*.

13 Since the cypresses were black, C is unlikely and their dry location makes B equally unlikely. A* is the correct answer though D would have been a reasonable though inaccurate deduction.

14 C* is correct. The word "aspect" here means "appearance". Cypress trees tend to grow in Mediterranean countries. A, B and D are complete red-herrings.

15 You may have wanted to include D* in the list of things done by the nun who comes to speak to Toby. In fact she merely approaches him and he backs away of his own accord. The only thing that is "sweeping" is her long clothes (line 59).

16 Toby's "distracted glance" gives way to his focussing on the nun's face, so A and D are inappropriate. Nor was he wilfully avoiding looking at her for we are told that he was watching her approach. So C is wrong and B* is the only possible answer here.

17 "Alarm" (line 73) implies fear (A); "desperate" (line 80) implies hopelessness (B); Toby's "agony of embarrassment" (line 73) must partake of shame (C), which leaves D*, for it is clear that Toby is in no real mood to respond to the beauty of the cemetery.

18 The answer must be A* for there is nothing malicious about the way the nun deals with Toby. She tries to be wholly considerate of his feelings and merely wants him to feel better before he leaves.

19 As in the answer to question 18, this is another example of the nun's attempt to make Toby feel better about his trespass. So D* would be the correct answer.

20 Toby ran down the avenue to get away from the enclosure and his curses are all directed towards himself. So B* must be the correct combination.

B   The Proposal

 1 There is no evidence of Stockdale pursuing any occupation in this passage but he is referred to as "the minister" at the start of the second paragraph. So, B* is correct and if you have opted for A or C, then you may have confused Stockdale with other characters mentioned in the passage.

 2 The crucial evidence comes around line 20 where we are told that Stockdale was merely someone who loved Lizzie and stood in no closer relationship to her than that. D* would, therefore, be most appropriate.

 3 From what Lizzie goes on to assert later in the passage and from her concern that their conversation may have been overheard, it is clear that she and Owlett were talking about A*.

 4 C* must be the answer. We can eliminate B and D because both imply noisy utterances and we are told that Lizzie spoke

in "low tones" (line 3). A is specifically denied by Lizzie.

5 To answer this question you need to understand "alternately low and firm" (line 10), which corresponds to 4, and "sometimes it reached the point of positive entreaty" (line 10), which is closest to 2. So D* is correct.

6 B* is correct. The conversation was not loud enough to constitute a row.

7 C is incorrect. The phrase refers to Stockdale and the fact that elsewhere he openly condemned the smuggling activity implies that B and D are inaccurate. A* is the closest definition.

8 D* is the only alternative that is not applicable to Stockdale's actions and feelings in the second paragraph.

9 Lizzie trusts Stockdale and so B cannot be right. She denies A and shows no evidence at all of being annoyed with Stockdale. So C* is the most likely.

10 The answer is A*. A "preoccupation" is a thought that occupies the mind to the exclusion of other ideas.

11 The clue is in lines 41–42 where Stockdale shows that he suspects they have been talking about love and marriage (C*).

12 B* is the one thing that Stockdale is not interested in.

13 B* is correct. In lines 50–52, Lizzie shows that she sees real danger in her conversation being overheard. So A, C and D are irrelevant.

14 Lizzie does not immediately change the subject (A) when Stockdale proposes to her but she does not give him a clear answer either. Her final promise to Stockdale is taken by him to be some sort of encouragement (D*) as is her allowing him to hold her hand.

15 A* is closest in meaning.

16 The whole atmosphere of the passage suggests that the story happened earlier than this century. So D cannot be correct. B might be associated with the miller but are unlikely to be

smuggled. There is no reason why A should be packed in tubs and C* is the traditional stuff of smuggling.

17 C* must be his concern. She is working with Owlett, so D will be unlikely. There would be no shame in B and there is no evidence in the passage that Stockdale thinks of Lizzie as a flirtatious woman.

18 B* is the answer; the taxes being avoided are import duty.

19 The evidence is in lines 79–80 and 88–89 where Lizzie tells Stockdale that she did not wish to offend her neighbours (A*).

20 It is true that Lizzie has given Stockdale her hand to hold earlier in the passage but D* is the reason for his looking happier at the very end of the passage.

C   Sarah Burton Examines Her Conscience

1 Although Miss Burton may appear to be carrying out the functions of the school secretary as she sorts her mail, it is clear that she is a person of senior authority in the school. The fact that she has a disciplinary role makes her more likely to be B or C* than A but her control of staffing arrangements and appointment of Miss Vane to replace Miss Sigglesthwaite clearly indicate her position as Headmistress.

2 D* is the answer. We are, it is true, told that she neglects her friends but this is the result of preoccupation with the school rather than unfriendliness. We see that she works quickly (C), makes decisions about the categories the letters fall into (B) and her speed and precision imply efficiency (A).

3 The first dash might be replaced by a colon since it introduces a list, but colons would be inappropriate in the two other places. Brackets might enclose the whole of the material after "contents" to the end of the sentence but would not be of any use in dividing up the items in the list. Semi-colons would imply too major a division between these simple phrases. Therefore, the comma (A*) is the only punctuation mark applicable to all three positions and would be correctly used.

4 You can get some clue as to the word's meaning from the context in which it is used. It follows a sentence that emphasizes

76

Miss Burton's particular concern. A "monomaniac" is some-one irrationally, madly preoccupied with one thing and so C* would be the most appropriate answer.

5 You need to be aware of the tone, the manner in which the phrase might have been uttered. It is a well-used saying but not so casual as to be slang. It is not exaggerated because Miss Burton does not mean it literally. Sarcasm implies biting criticism of someone or something and that is not the case here. So D* is most appropriate: Miss Burton uses an image, a metaphor, to express an idea.

6 Miss Burton feels she has "treated Miss Sigglesthwaite shabbily" so A is applicable and so is D, especially when we note the last sentence of the paragraph. C is only another way of saying that "she had given her rope to hang herself". Although she blames herself for replacing Miss Sigglesthwaite, there is no reason to suppose that she thinks Miss Vane an inadequate substitute. So B* is the answer.

7 The clues are mainly in lines 69–73. Although they have opened up a new world to Miss Sigglesthwaite, these novels are clearly not science fiction, nor are they about fashion, although underwear comes into them, and the conflict of virtue with vice (D) is only part of the main subject (B*) suggested in "the declaration of love" (line 71).

8 The clue is in line 74 and A* is correct. Miss Burton is B. C is Miss Sigglesthwaite's present post and D could only be a mis-understanding of line 74.

9 In the letter, B is but briefly referred to in passing and, although the other alternatives are elements in it, the letter does turn into a long expression of gratitude (A*).

10 Lines 75–6 offer the clearest statement of Miss Burton's feelings and B* sums them up. Her thoughtfulness, her admiration for Miss Sigglesthwaite as a scientist and her concern for her new way of life are all part of the wider feeling of guilt.

11 If your answer is D*, you are closest to the meaning. Her philosophy may well have been rejuvenating and reliable but neither is what the word actually means. A is the opposite of its meaning.

12 Both D and B* are good definitions but B is more literally what the word means, picking up the idea of not ceasing or not restraining her efforts.

13 Since the punctuation mark separates two sentences dealing with very similar material, A or B* are possible alternatives. But the second sentence does not explain the first so they could be regarded as parallel statements about a closely related topic and so be divided by a semi-colon.

14 If you have opted for A, you may not have been thinking generally enough: getting rid of Miss Sigglesthwaite was only a short-term project and the question asks what Miss Burton's mind was *always* planning. If you have opted for D, you have been less precise than you might be for we are told in lines 7–8 that C* was Miss Burton's preoccupation.

15 This question requires you to summarize your understanding of Miss Sigglesthwaite's character. Miss Burton acknowledges her generosity (line 77) and to describe her as a distinguished scientist implies that she was cultured, as does Miss Sigglesthwaite's own elegant letter (D). Miss Burton also pictures her untidy appearance (C). In no sense does Miss Sigglesthwaite reproach Miss Burton (B*) for her treatment of her.

16 You must read carefully and respond to the whole paragraph. A and D are obviously true: they are Miss Burton's positive attempt to help Miss Sigglesthwaite. B is likewise true: although she was trying to help the unhappy woman, she was also thinking about the school. C* is not true: Miss Burton had felt some impatience (line 90) but had not generally been impatient.

17 A and D are incorrect. Miss Burton did not speak out loud at all (C). B* is the closest.

18 You need to put information from lines 22–3 together with the paragraph beginning line 77 in order to answer this question. The teacher who took Miss Sigglesthwaite's place (B) was Miss Vane (line 21). Midge Carne's unhealthy influence was emotional not physical (C). There is no evidence for A and so we may deduce that D* is correct: Midge Carne was the ringleader of line 23.

19 B and D might be possible answers but based solely on
speculation, not on given information. A and C* are both
correct but the latter is far more precise. It says the same as the
final sentence of the passage: that Joe helped her retain her
self-respect.

20 The author does not condemn Miss Burton (A) nor does she
make any judgement about D: implied in the passage are
arguments for and against the replacement of Miss Sigglesthwaite. C may or may not be the view of the author but we
do not know how she might judge Miss Burton as a headmistress. In fact, the author's concern to show how Miss
Burton is too ready to condemn herself (B*) emerges throughout the passage from line 77 onwards and Miss Sigglesthwaite's
letter shows how kind and considerate Miss Burton had been.

Chapter 3

A Shooting an Elephant

1 Later in the passage Orwell explores the idea of what might
have happened had the elephant charged him, but even then
he denies any feeling of fear. In this first paragraph there is no
mention at all of B*.

2 He certainly decides not to kill the elephant at present but that
does not mean that the killing is merely postponed (A). He
would watch him for a while but not with the intention of then
killing him (B), nor is he completely rejecting the possibility
of ever killing him (C). D* is the answer.

3 This metaphor expresses the author's sense that the elephant
is useful (1), valuable (5) and superbly made (3), a wonder of
the natural world just as a great machine is a man-made
wonder. So C* must be correct.

4 In spite of its casual expression, C* is the answer. The crowd
was fascinated by the presence of the rifle and had gathered
to watch the diverting spectacle. A and D are too specialized
to be relevant and there is no evidence in this paragraph of B.
Moreover, we are told a few lines earlier that the crowd was
"happy and excited over this bit of fun."

5 The clue in the passage is in the sentences that follow. The

author felt the enormous pressure of the will of the crowd (A*). He specifically denies C elsewhere in the passage, has already said that D was not the case and B cannot be true for the rest of the paragraph is all about what a false position he felt himself to be in.

6 The crucial words are "futility" meaning pointlessness and "dominion" meaning power or control. So C* is the closest definition of the phrase and the alternatives all bring in irrelevant material.

7 Both B and D suggest the falseness of Orwell's position but only B* suggests that his power depends entirely on the will of others.

8 A* is the nearest in meaning. The word implies some disapproval.

9 To be "squeamish" means to be sickened by something and so C* is the answer. However, the other possibilities could have been eliminated from evidence elsewhere in the passage.

10 You must look at the sentence that precedes the quoted phrase in order to see that C* must be the answer, that is, Orwell's plan to test the reactions of the elephant by walking to within twenty-five yards of him.

11 A and B cannot be correct for "natives" is a common enough word and although one might well put a slang word in inverted commas, that is not the case here. In fact, Orwell is using the word ironically so as to prompt us to see what associations we have with the word "natives" (D*).

12 The one thing that the author specifically denies is that he was frightened (line 59), whereas he acknowledges that he was "a poor shot" (A) and that he would be unlikely to escape a charge from close quarters (B). Above all he was concerned not to give the natives an opportunity to laugh (D). So C* is the correct choice.

13 Although Orwell fears creating a spectacle of amusement (B*), he has not done so yet.

14 Line 74 defines the part of the head to be aimed at. It is an

imaginary line between the ear-holes that would pass through where the elephant's brain is and C* is the reason why he should have aimed there, so as to have killed him instantly.

15 A* is, perhaps surprisingly, the answer as the author tells us in the comment included in dashes on line 80.

16 The main part of the sentence from which the quotation is taken continues, after a little aside, with "even for the bullet to get there". So B* is correct.

17 Although any of the suggested words might fill the slot occupied by "senility", "aging" (A*) is the most accurate definition, as the sentence that follows the phrase indicates.

18 The elephant's collapse (A) occurs after a pause (line 88) and his attempt to get up (D) occurs after the author has fired his second shot. C was no change and B* is the answer as shown in line 86.

19 The visible jet of agony through the elephant (D), his trumpeting (A) and falling (B) are all recorded in the final paragraph. So C* must be the answer.

20 The question is simpler than it appears. Items 1 and 3 are not present in this paragraph. Orwell is most likely to have had his weight and size in mind and D* would be correct.

B The Tea Shop

1 This is a metaphor which compares the lights of London's West End with fountains that throw out their water just as the lights scatter "illumination". D* is the best description.

2 A "citadel" is a defended outpost, a fortress (A*) as is suggested in the phrases that follow.

3 You need to respond to the humorous tone of the writer. The extreme alternatives of a "new civilisation" or "new barbarism" suggest that he takes the whole thing with a pinch of salt (C*).

4 C* is the answer. The full comparison is between the superficial marble front of the building that hides the concrete and steel structure and the appearance of careless luxury that hides the

fact that this is a carefully controlled business that must make a profit.

5 C is obviously wrong, unless you were put off by the reference to the basement being used for administration and, although the author lists the many people working in the building, he never infers B. The correct answer is the opposite of D for the author is asserting that somewhere, someone is organizing the tea shop down to the last detail and that organization is necessary because the tea shop is there to be a successful business (A*).

6 D* is the item not included in the first paragraph. That comes later when Turgis encounters the large number of people in the entrance hall.

7 The clue is presented in lines 26 and 27: Turgis sought "all the enchantment of unfamiliar luxury". C* is therefore the answer.

8 B and D may well be true statements but the author indicates why he had chosen this particular comparison in the words that precede it. Both places would be crowded and bustling (A*).

9 Any of the words suggested could fill a slot left by "disdaining" but if you caught the association of disapproval and assertion of superiority in that word, then you will have chosen C*.

10 The violinist has "lustrous" or shining eyes; his drawing of the girls like a magnet might be called "sex appeal"; "tremolo effects" are quavering sounds full of feeling; the only quality listed here which Priestley does not ascribe to him is poor playing (B*).

11 D* was the only item not noticed by Turgis as he entered the restaurant. His own anxiety to be served came later.

12 It was the suddenness of the sound that Turgis was aware of as the door opened and "sugary" suggests the sweet attractiveness that the whole building offered him. The other associations of bombs are hardly relevant here. So C* must be the answer.

13 B* is the closest in meaning to "deferentially".

14 The tone of A* catches the level of Turgis's feelings. He is not

experiencing extreme conflicts nor painful tensions but we are told that he is feeling something, that is, shy and proud.

15 This is a different type of question, directing you to the manner in which the content of the passage has been written. The last paragraph begins with a couple of very conversational statements, just the sort of thing that Turgis might have said and so B* gives the most appropriate reason for the change of style.

16 We know that Turgis enjoyed all the noise and bustle of the tea shop so 1 cannot be correct. There is no evidence that he was disapproving of people at nearby tables: he merely regretted that none of the attractive girls were taking any notice of him. The fact that the ladies at his table were eating cream cakes is irrelevant to his annoyance. D* is the correct answer: his initial irritation with having to sit where he was put (2) was increased by the poor service (5).

17 The answer must be C*, as the evidence in lines 58–60 proves.

18 Given his concern with their "saucy eyes and wide smiling mouths" (line 74), we may safely assume that B* is the answer.

19 "Amorous" means loving and D* must be correct.

20 Turgis would have been quite happy to wait for his tea if one of the attractive girls in the vicinity had begun to take some notice of him. That is his main preoccupation in this last paragraph and so C* is a better answer than B or D. A is inaccurate.

C Sunday Morning Life on the Common

1 A "distinction" here means a distinctively different quality and since the author refers to "Sunday morning" rather than to one specific day, C* must be correct. The author makes this clear in lines 8–11 where she begins to define the particular quality of "Sunday morning".

2 A* must be correct. An access is an approach or entry and something "inaccessible" must be impossible to get to.

3 An "observance" is keeping a law or following a custom, here the customs of life on the Common. "Observation" meaning seeing is entirely different from "observance" and you have been misled by the similarity between the two words if you

opted for A or D. C is a red-herring and B* is the answer.

4 Lines 9 and 10 make it clear that D* must be the answer. The Commoners have nothing to do with God and the other experiences of the Sunday are listed in lines 10–14.

5 A* is the only answer that offers a definition of the phrase but you will have been able to deduce that it has something to do with the past from the lines that follow immediately after it.

6 B* is the closest definition.

7 Common sense will suggest that C* must be the answer. The people living in this area are wealthy enough to be able to afford to send their children to fee-paying boarding schools.

8 Close reading of the preceding sentence makes clear that "they" must refer to the *au pair* girls who do the cooking and have their own social life among themselves (D*).

9 The use of Christian names by the cooks means that D is inappropriate. The employers want to have friendly relationships with them. There is no suggestion of disrespect and the sherry is "pressed upon them": they have not taken to the bottle! So B* must be the answer.

10 In a cuckoo-clock, a small mechanical bird emerges on the hour to indicate the time, so A* is the answer since it brings in the idea of regular occurrence and also the sentence begins with reference to "noon".

11 You may have chosen "writers" (B), not realizing that "playwrights" are specialized writers. The only possibility of which there is no mention in the list given in lines 28–33 is "clergymen" (D*).

12 The key to answering this question correctly is in the phrase, "their tenure less secure". It indicates an insecurity, an uncertainty on the part of this category of Commoner as to whether they really ought to be part of this community. In line 49 we are told that success is the main concern of the men and so the insecurity of these men must relate to success (A*).

13 In line 28 we are invited to watch the front doors of the houses

(1) and in line 38 an aerial view (4) is suggested. So A* must be correct.

14 Visiting (B) takes place after noon. It is only the less secure residents who look to see if weeds are appearing on their gravel drives (A). D is not even mentioned but the imaginary aerial view would reveal the man in his garden with the newspaper on the ground nearby (C*).

15 B and D *may* be true statements though A is unlikely and C* catches the meaning of "conform", to do what everyone else is doing.

16 A, C and D contain inaccuracies but B* most clearly summarizes the paragraph.

17 If you have the correct interpretation of the fifth paragraph, you will have no trouble with this question. The tension felt by women whose lives are unfulfilled is expressed in the statement quoted. Nothing as simple and literal as A, C or D is adequate here. B* is the answer.

18 The words that come before these in the passage make it clear that it is "the hosts for this morning" (A*) that remain in their houses.

19 The smooth running of the cars (1) and their shining appearance (4) are the qualities brought out in comparing them with marbles. 2 cannot be relevant for the cars are not small and 3 has nothing to do with marbles. D* is correct.

20 The whole sentence makes clear the meaning of "heretic". In this context it would be someone who did not attend the drinks party and who does not believe in the value of this corporate activity (D*). Just as people in church take bread and wine in the communion service, so the author wittily suggests that this community has its own ritual and what is eaten and drunk is rather like bread and wine.

Chapter 4

A The Trade Unions and Industrial Change

1 The sentence preceding the first use of the word "Luddism" in the passage offers an example of workers destroying new

85

machinery (A*). The meaning can, therefore, be deduced from the context even though you may not know anything about the original Luddites.

2 C* is the best summary statement of the content of this first paragraph. The author wants to introduce the idea of unions opposing changes in industry by striking, a tactic he calls "neo-Luddism".

3 The Railway Brotherhood, in its insistence that unnecessary workers continue in employment, certainly did not promote efficiency (A), nor were they successful in opposing the introduction of the diesel engine (B). It was not a question of employing additional staff (C) but rather of maintaining existing levels of employment by retaining firemen when they were no longer necessary (D*).

4 B* is the central point of the paragraph: the need to maintain industrial development. A is not asserted for the author merely expresses sympathy with the unemployed skilled worker and C and D are subsidiary arguments giving added weight to the central argument of the paragraph.

5 Man-made fibres (C*) have not declined. The growth of their manufacture has caused decline in cotton and woollen industries.

6 He specifies the development of air transport (1) and the increased capacity of other countries to build their own ships (3) as reasons for the decline of shipbuilding. So C* is correct.

7 In the theatre, the actor who holds the centre of the stage is the star, someone acknowledged to be a master of his profession. So C* is the most appropriate choice.

8 B* is the answer. To be wary is to be anticipating some danger in a fearful way.

9 The fear of the workers (A) will not help industrial change, nor will the unions' desire to protect their members (C) at the expense of cooperating with management. D* must be the answer here.

10 B* is the closest definition. The idea of changing (D) is not

contained within the word "techniques" which refers to skills rather than the machines which allow for them to be practised (A and C).

11 B is quite close but D* captures the idea behind the use of the word in this context. The unions' automatic reaction to new machinery is concern for their own jobs.

12 The answer occurs in the rest of the sentence on line 46. It is a quarrel between unions representing different types of skill that constitutes a "demarcation dispute" (D*).

13 The arguments against allowing rigid demarcations to apply in people's jobs are given in lines 50–51, which neatly summarize A, C and D. The author makes no mention of a poorer quality product being the result (B*).

14 "This" must refer to the main idea of the previous sentence which is concerned with the loyalties of the unions. C* is the closest definition offered here. B occurs too early in the paragraph to be directly related.

15 As a result of strikes by printing unions, some companies have had to close, so A* is the answer. The paragraph is concerned with the self-destructiveness that results from unions opposing the introduction of new techniques.

16 Lines 67 and 68 identify the answer, which is the loss of jobs and the saving of labour (B*).

17 The point being made is that there is likely to be less opposition to the introduction of automation in *new* industries, of which electronics is an example (C*).

18 B* is the answer. The "it" in line 68 also refers back to "This very advanced form of mechanisation" in the previous sentence.

19 "Predictable" (C) is close but "unavoidable" (B*) or "bound to happen" is a closer definition of "inevitable".

20 The whole tendency of the argument is directed towards the final statement, a plea to the trade unions to be more adaptable and open to new ideas. So D* is correct.

B   Television Reporting and Newspaper Reporting

1 The first five questions are designed to help you summarize this passage and grasp how the argument develops. The author begins by recording the relative ease in practical terms that he has experienced when turning from television to newspaper reporting (D*).

2 In the second paragraph, he details the more practical disadvantages of television reporting (A and B) but says that far more important ("What counts . . ." line 18) is the psychological fact that the interviewee is more reluctant to speak freely in front of a television camera (C*).

3 This short paragraph continues the author's consideration of the methods of recording interviews and the first sentence introduces its subject: the notebook as recording equipment. The point the author goes on to make about the use of the notebook is that the interviewee forgets about its presence and that helps him to be less self-conscious (D*).

4 The paragraph begins with further advantages to be derived from not using a notebook at all until the interview is over. This allows for a much easier flow of questions and answers during the interview. The author then points out that the one disadvantage of simply remembering everything that was said is that you cannot then quote exactly what the subject said and you miss having the use of some of his most interesting statements. So, although B, C and D are all mentioned in the course of the paragraph, only A* sums it all up.

5 Finally, the author takes up the problem of being unable to use the subject's most interesting statements and relates this idea back to television reporting. The fact is that television reporters are unable to make any use of the more relaxed and indiscreet comments that a subject might make just after an interview has finished (B*). A is a subsidiary point to the fuller statement in B*. C is not an issue in the paragraph and D amplifies A.

6 A is close but C* captures the sense of writing having greater weight than pictorial reporting.

7 D* must be the answer as the rest of the paragraph makes clear. The author is specifically talking about newspaper reporting, not publishing in general.

8 He mentions that, as a newspaper reporter, he is on his own (line 7); he has no camera crew (line 8); and no longer needs "more than a dozen bulky boxes" (line 11). He nowhere mentions that he is fitter (B*) which would be an irrelevance to his argument.

9 A is not applicable to the task and C and D, though probably relevant, are only aspects of the nearest meaning given here: laborious (B*).

10 Dismissing this complex process of technology with the flippant word "rigmarole", implies that the author is regarding the whole thing humorously (C*).

11 B* is not specified as being necessary. "Telephones" (line 14) are mentioned in connection with the work of the newspaper reporter.

12 Lines 22–25 identify the feelings of the man being interviewed by a television reporter. A, B and D are all feelings or pre-occupations that he may have. C* is the answer, for the author is saying that the last thing the interviewee will be doing is talking naturally with the interviewer.

13 The "It" that begins the sentence refers back to a previous statement, that the subject is self-conscious "if there is a camera behind you" (line 21). So A* is the answer.

14 A* is the closest definition. The notebook appears very innocent.

15 D is incorrect: the use of the tape-recorder would be more appropriate to the television reporter. The person who "forgets" the notebook is the subject being interviewed, not the reporter (C). A is true as a statement but lines 31–32 give the reason for not using the notebook (B*).

16 C* is the answer.

17 The author is not scorning (D*) the people he interviews, though he is being slightly condescending (C) in tone. The word conveys a little more than its obvious meaning which must include A and B.

18 A simile, or direct comparison, is effective if it crystallizes the author's main idea which here is the ability to remember all of an interview and reproduce it later. So D* is the answer.

19 "Anonymously" means without using one's name. So A* is correct.

20 C* is the answer. A, B and D may be true but line 47 specifies the author's reservation about the "chipmunk" method of reporting: it is not precise enough because you do not record exactly what the subject says.

21 The author is saying that the reporter can only quote damaging statements made by a subject if he allows his name to be attached to them. B* is the answer. It could also have been arrived at by eliminating the others.

22 B, C and D may or may not be true but A* is the reason for his being mentioned, along with the backbencher (line 52).

23 You have to be aware of the sentence structure here. The phrase refers back to the previous paragraph where the author was giving typical examples of the interesting things people say when they are more relaxed. So C* is the closest summary.

24 A* is clearly the impression given in lines 55–57.

25 The "it" in line 57, the thing that television reporters cannot use, refers back to the previous sentence, to "that kind of observation" which, in turn, refers back to D* as question 23 made clear.

C The Case For and Against Small Primary Schools

1 D* is the most precise definition of "This movement" which refers back to the first sentence of the extract. B is a specific example of this change and C is a more general statement.

2 The "sceptics", we are told, think that the main cause of changes in the organization of rural schools has been the need to save money. They are not impressed by the more educational reasons that are put forward and A* is the most appropriate of the definitions offered. The more usual meaning of "sceptic" is someone who disbelieves in a religion.

3 The answer has nothing to do with a political party (D), nor with the work teachers do (C), nor the salaries they earn (A). A larger number of small schools means more teachers proportionate to the number of children being taught. So B* is correct.

4 The economic reason (3) has already been mentioned. The cost of staffing has led to the reduction in the number of primary schools. The other influence, the educational reason, is the partial carrying out of the Gittins report which proposed that the minimum size for a primary school be 60 pupils (2). C* is the answer.

5 The distinction is between the theory – the closure of all schools of less than 60 pupils as advised by Gittins – and the practice, which is less extreme in its application. A* is the most appropriate.

6 "The pace" is a continuation of the metaphor of change implied in the "movement" of question 1. Again it refers back to the opening sentence of the passage of which B* is a summary.

7 D* is the answer. In the passage we are told that the curriculum now includes various new subjects. The context should have helped you work out the right answer to this question.

8 A* is the answer. The author, having introduced the topic of equipment and materials, brushes aside the question of their cost in order to deal with the issue of what space might be available in the school for their storage and use.

9 The nearest meaning is D*. Children in such small rural schools would, the author suggests, not enjoy the advantages, the benefits, of studying subjects that might be available in larger schools.

10 This question summarizes the main points of the second paragraph: children could be disadvantaged if their teachers were unable to offer them a full range of subjects (1), and the buildings themselves are inadequate for housing the equipment required in modern schools (4). The author deliberately avoids the question of costs (2), as we saw in the previous question, and 3 is not mentioned in the paragraph. C* is correct.

11 The word means that there would be no change if the school were so small that only one teacher worked there. D* is correct.

12 The question requires you to think out the meaning of "urban standards of education" (line 40) which is what the townspeople want. B* is the nearest equivalent, "urban" simply meaning "of the town".

13 If you have answered the last couple of questions correctly, this one should pose no problem. 3 and 5 are the main arguments put forward against small rural schools in this paragraph (C*).

14 A "proponent" is someone who puts forward a theory or proposal. A, B and C all imply opposition to small schools. Only D* identifies proponents as supporters of the idea.

15 C* must be correct as the continuation of the sentence shows. They are places where "children of different ages help each other".

16 "This" here must be "vertically grouped classes", the teaching of younger children by older pupils (B*).

17 C* may be true in country village schools but it is not actually mentioned in this sentence. All the other reasons are included.

18 The reference to "transporting one person" (line 60) should have given you the clue if you did not already know the meaning of this word. A* is the closest definition.

19 A has been denied earlier in the extract and B is hardly a reason for preferring the existence of small schools – merely in order to change them into something else. D may possibly be true but is not presented so specifically in this final sentence of the extract. C* is a summary of why the administrator may prefer small schools.

20 This is difficult to decide: the author gives convincing reasons both for retaining small schools and for merging them with larger schools. Although he does counter some of the objections to small schools, for example by suggesting that peripatetic teachers could cover the wider curriculum re-

quired, he leaves others unanswered. On balance, he seems a little more in favour of small schools; that is the argument he leaves us with at the end of the passage. However, his aim is obviously not propaganda and, even if he does have his own view, he wants the various points to speak for themselves. So, A* seems the best description of his aim.

D   The Aims and Purposes of the Social Services

1 "Statutory" refers to statutes or laws and so C* is the closest definition. It would, of course, follow that such institutions would be officially recognized (D) but that is a result not the essential fact of their existence.

2 The phrase "but so too" clearly divides the sentence in half and separates the two sorts of "services" provided in the community between which he distinguishes. The first half of the sentence refers to poor relief of various sorts and the second half to services which help everyone. So B* summarizes the distinction.

3 A* is the closest definition offered here. To distinguish something is to see clearly its identity, to see what makes it different.

4 In lines 5–7, the author gives a sequence of examples of social services that benefit everyone and he does not include unemployment benefit (D*) which, it is obvious, is beneficial only to the unemployed.

5 This question summarizes the main point of the first paragraph, which is concerned to define the nature of the social services. It is all summed up in the final sentence of the paragraph which identifies the social services with individual well-being (C*).

6 The context of the sentence implies that A* is the answer.

7 Adam Smith was concerned to make the point that people only sell things in order to make a profit, the motive being self-interest, not desire to give charity to others. So C* is the answer.

8 The question may be answered by looking at the previous sentence to see what "This" refers to. D is an idea only intro-

duced later in the paragraph. Likewise B occurs later and is, in any case, a misreading of the reference to butchers. C is, indeed, an idea from the previous sentence but it is incidental to the main idea: the motive behind the provision of commercial services. So A* must be correct.

9   The question requires you to come to terms with the last two sentences of the paragraph. These revert to the idea at the end of the first paragraph. B* is the answer. A and D are only distantly implied here and C is specifically dismissed by the author as not being his concern.

10 The author gives the answer in the remainder of the sentence from which the question is taken. D* is a recasting of that idea.

11 The main idea is B*. C and D are more detailed examples of the main point.

12 A* is the answer. D is close but does not include the idea of ceasing or sudden loss of something.

13 "contingencies" are chance happenings. So A* is the closest definition.

14 The particular application of this phrase is made clear in the previous sentence which directly uses the words of B*.

15 You need to have taken in the whole of this paragraph to deal with this question. The question asked by the author in this connection comes in lines 65–67 and is expressed more simply in C*.

16 The author contradicts A, does not mention B and introduces C with reference to wealthy parents in general. D* is the answer: millionaires, along with the poorest members of the Community, may benefit from National Health Services.

17 A is not even mentioned in the fifth paragraph and would contradict a major point that the author is making. B is an idea introduced in connection with the relationship between millionaires and the National Health Service. D is fantasy and C* is stated in lines 73–74.

18 C* is the answer. 1 merely restates the last half of the sentence whilst 4 refers to the first half.

19 The previous part of the statement provides the answer which is restated in D*. B is a very garbled version of the point the author goes on to make. C, though a central idea in the passage, is not referred to at this point and A is not true.

20 In the final sentence, the author is dealing with a misconception which is summed up by A*.

Key Facts Educational Aids

KEY FACTS PASSCARDS

Additional Mathematics
Algebra
Arithmetic & Trigonometry
Biology
Chemistry
Computer Studies
Economics
Elementary Mathematics
English Comprehension
English Language
French
General Science

Geography
Geography British Isles
Geometry
German
History (1815-1914)
History (1914-1951)
Human Biology
Modern Mathematics
New Testament
Physics
Technical Drawing

KEY FACTS COURSE COMPANIONS

Additional Mathematics
Algebra
Arithmetic & Trigonometry
Biology
Chemistry
Economics

English
French
Geography
Geometry
Modern Mathematics
Physics

KEY FACTS A-LEVEL BOOKS

Biology
Chemistry

Physics
Pure Mathematics

KEY FACTS O-LEVEL PASSBOOKS

Biology
Chemistry
Computer Studies
Economics
English Language
French
Geography

Geography British Isles
History (Political & Constitutional)
History (Social & Economic)
Human Biology
Modern Mathematics
Physics
Technical Drawing

KEY FACTS A-LEVEL PASSBOOKS

Applied Mathematics
Biology
Chemistry
Economics

Geography
Physics
Pure Mathematics
Pure & Applied Mathematics

KEY FACTS O-LEVEL MODEL ANSWERS

Biology
Chemistry
English Language
French

Geography
History (Social & Economic)
Modern Mathematics
Physics

KEY FACTS REFERENCE LIBRARY

Biology
Chemistry
Geography

History (1815-1914)
Physics
Traditional Mathematics

KEY FACTS O-LEVEL MULTIPLE CHOICE

Biology
Chemistry
Economics
English
French
Geography

Geography British isles
History (Social & Economic)
Human Biology
Modern Mathematics
Physics

KEY FACTS A-LEVEL WORKED EXAMPLES

Applied Mathematics
Biology
Chemistry
Economics

Geography
Physics
Pure Mathematics
Pure & Applied Mathematics

KEY FACTS DICTIONARIES

Biology
Chemistry
Economics

Geography
Mathematics
Physics